BEST of the BEST
from
SOUTH CAROLINA

Selected Recipes from South Carolina's
FAVORITE COOKBOOKS

Wendy & Kiernan,

    I know how much both of you enjoy cooking. I hope you will find wonderful South Carolina recipes herein that will become some of your favorites to prepare.

    Happy Anniversary to two of my favorite people in the whole world.

                Mom

June 2000

BEST
of the BEST
from
SOUTH
CAROLINA

Selected Recipes from South Carolina's
FAVORITE COOKBOOKS

EDITED BY

Gwen McKee

AND

Barbara Moseley

Illustrated by Tupper Davidson

QUAIL RIDGE PRESS

Best of the best from South Carolina: selected recipes from South Carolina's favorite cookbooks / edited by Gwen McKee and Barbara Moseley; illustrated by Tupper Davidson.
  p. cm.
  Includes index.
  ISBN 0-937552-39-9: $14.95
  1. Cookery—South Carolina. 2. Cookery, American—Southern sytle.
I. McKee, Gwen. II. Moseley, Barbara.
TX715.B485642 1990   90-42214
641.59757—dc20   CIP

First printing, October 1990; Second, February 1992;
Third, January 1994; Fourth, November 1997; Fifth, January 1999
Manufactured in the United States of America
Chapter opening photos and cover photo courtesy of
South Carolina Division of Tourism, City of Sumter and Thoroughbred Country
QUAIL RIDGE PRESS
P.O. Box 123 • Brandon, MS 39043 • 1-800-343-1583

CONTENTS

Editors Gwen McKee and Barbara Moseley getting their feet wet on Myrtle Beach.

PREFACE

If there was one word to describe South Carolina, it would have to be "charm." It is a state that literally charms you with its quaint old buildings, its islands and inlets, its azaleas and irises, its thoroughbreds and vineyards. No wonder the leading industry in the state (besides textiles) is tourism! No doubt about it, from Upcountry to Lowcountry, all through South Carolina, we were entirely charmed.

And no surprise at all that the food was equally as charming ... and delicious! Though Charleston and the coast are most often thought about when one thinks of South Carolina, our research proved that the Palmetto State is interesting and fascinating from border to border. Along the Atlantic coast—from Myrtle Beach to Hilton Head Island—the creatures of the sea find their way into huge restaurant pots as well as backyard smokers, producing delicacies that one doesn't soon forget. Famous for She-Crab Soup, Oysters Purlo, Huguenot Tortes, and Carolina Red Rice, South Carolinians also brag that they make the best pecan pie, deviled crab and benne wafers in the world. And who could argue?

We can say without reservation that the forty-eight contributors to this volume have also been charming, lending us their favorite recipes along with their enthusiasm and support. We are indeed grateful to the authors, editors, and publishers for their cooperation in making this book possible. Each contributing cookbook has its own special features— pictures, artwork, anecdotes, history, cooking hints, calorie counts, etc.—and we have attempted to retain their flavors by reproducing the recipes as they appear in each book, changing only typeset style for uniformity. The complete catalog showing and describing each book, along with ordering information begins on page 269. Cooks and collectors interested in exploring the tastes and styles of South Carolina will want

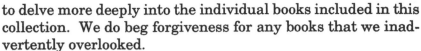

to delve more deeply into the individual books included in this collection. We do beg forgiveness for any books that we inadvertently overlooked.

There is an arduous amount of research and work that goes into compiling this book, and we could not do it without help from old friends and new acquaintances. Tupper Davidson has an uncanny knack for coming up with appropriate artwork that adds so much to the spirit of the book. And Sheila Williams and Annette Goode were always willing to sort, separate, fold, stamp—whatever was required. Our sincere thanks go to all the food editors from newspapers across the state who recommended cookbooks for inclusion, the book and gift store managers who thoughtfully lent their knowledge of popular books from their areas, the folks at the tourism department who provided us with pictures and information, and especially the people of South Carolina we met along the way who were always so eager to chat and share good news as well as food news.

We are extremely pleased to present these lovely South Carolina cookbooks and their outstanding recipes. It is our hope that we have captured some of the traditions and tastes of the state, and that herein perhaps you too can experience as we did—the unmatchable charm of South Carolina. Enjoy!

Gwen McKee and Barbara Moseley

Contributing Cookbooks

Bethel Food Bazaar II
Bluffton's Favorite Recipes
Carolina Cuisine
Carolina Cuisine Encore!
Catch-of-the-Day
Charleston Receipts
Charleston Receipts Repeats
Charleston Recollections and Receipts
Cooking...Done the Baptist Way
Cooking on the Go
Culinary Crinkles
"Don't Forget the Parsley...."
The Enlightened Gourmet
Feeding the Faithful
500 Favorite Recipes
Flavored With Tradition
Hudson's Cookbook
Island Events Cookbook
A Journal of Fine Cooking
The Museum Cookbook
Nell Graydon's Cook Book
Olivia's Favorite Menus and Recipes
One Course At A Time
Palmetto Evenings
The Peach Sampler

Contributing Cookbooks

Please Don't Feed the Alligators
Pool Bar Jim's Famous Frozen Drinks
Prescriptions for Good Eating
Putting On The Grits
Recipes from Pawleys Island
The Sandlapper Cookbook
The Sandlappers' Salvation Cookbook
Sea Island Seasons
Seasoned with Light
The South Carolina Cook Book
South Carolina's Historic Restaurants
and their recipes
Southeastern Wildlife Cookbook
Southern Cooking
Southern Fish and Seafood Cookbook
Southern Vegetable Cooking
Southern Wildfowl and Wild Game Cookbook
Stir Crazy!
Stirrin' The Pots On Daufuskie
Strictly For Boys
A Taste of South Carolina
Thoroughbred Fare
Two Hundred Years of Charleston Cooking
Uptown Down South

Appetizers

Some of Charleston's beautifully preserved homes as seen through an ornate ironwork gate.

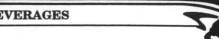

Peachy Twirl Cooler

3 medium peaches	2 tablespoons sugar
1 tablespoon lemon juice	1 cup milk
1 teaspoon almond extract	1 cup peach ice cream

Peel, pit, and slice peaches. Reserve 2 slices; dip in lemon juice. Place remainder of the sliced peaches in the blender and purée. Add lemon juice, almond extract, sugar and milk; cover and blend thoroughly. Mix in peach ice cream. Pour into large glasses; garnish each with reserved peach slice and a sprig of mint. Serve immediately. Makes two 12-ounce servings.

The Peach Sampler

Orange Ice

12 oranges	Water
4 lemons	4 egg whites per quart
Sugar	

To the juice of 12 oranges and 4 lemons, add as much water as will reduce it to the desired strength (as you do for lemonade). Then, make it very sweet. To each quart of this add the whites of 4 eggs beaten to a strong froth. Freeze very quickly.

Charleston Recollections and Receipts

South Carolina ranks among the nation's elite when it comes to training thoroughbreds. The horsy towns of Aiken and Camden have established an international reputation for their excellence as winter training grounds. Polo thrives in this area, along with harness racing and steeplechasing.

Wedding Punch

4 cups sugar
6 cups boiling water
1/4 cup tea leaves
1 cup lemon juice

3 cups pineapple juice
4 cups orange juice
6 quarts ginger ale

Combine sugar and 3 cups of boiling water. Stir until dissolved. Boil 7 minutes, cool. Pour remaining boiling water over tea leaves. Let stand 5 minutes, strain at once. Cool, then dilute with enough water to make one gallon. Combine fruit juices, sugar, syrup and diluted tea. Chill. Shortly before serving, pour over ice in punch bowl and add ginger ale. Lemon or orange slices, cherries or mint may be added if desired.

The South Carolina Cook Book

Dixie Tea

8 cups boiling water	2 cups sugar
5 tablespoons tea leaves	8 cups water
Juice of 1 lemon	1 teaspoon whole cloves
Juice of 6 oranges	

Add the boiling water to the tea, let stand five minutes and pour the tea off the leaves. Add the fruit juices and a syrup made by boiling the sugar, water and cloves to the tea. This makes about eighteen cups.

Two Hundred Years of Charleston Cooking

Hot Buttered Rum

Yummy, worth every calorie!

1 stick butter, melted	1 cup vanilla ice cream
1/2 cup plus 1 tablespoon brown sugar	24 ounces rum
1/2 cup plus 1 tablespoon white sugar	

Mix butter and sugars. Beat with rotary beater and add the ice cream by spoonfuls. This mixture may be stored for several days in the refrigerator.

To make drink, place 2 tablespoons of mixture in a cup and add 2 ounce jigger of rum. Fill with boiling water. Serves 12.

Calories 294.20, Protein 0.58gm, Fat 8.21gm, Carbohydrates 23.31gm, Fiber 0.00gm, Cholesterol 25.81mg, Saturated Fats 4.67gm, Iron 0.38mg, Calcium 27.96mg, Sodium 104.55mg, Potassium 61.47mg, Vitamin A 334.77 I.U., Vitamin C 0.11mg, Thiamine 0.01mg, Riboflavin 0.03mg, Niacin 0.03mg

The Enlightened Gourmet

 South Carolina boasts many universities: The University of South Carolina is located in Columbia; Clemson University is in Clemson; Furman University and Bob Jones University are in Greenville; The Citadel is in Charleston.

May Wine

1 cup fresh mint leaves
3/4 cup superfine sugar
3 liters California chenin
  blanc wine
2 bottles chilled California
  champagne

1 orange, thinly sliced
1 quart strawberries,
  cleaned and trimmed
1 cup fresh pineapple slices

Place mint, sugar, and 4 cups chenin blanc in a bowl, cover and chill overnight. Strain and pour into a large punch bowl over ice ring. Add remainder of chenin blanc, champagne, strawberries and pineapple.

Note: For an attractive ice ring, freeze some fresh mint leaves in water.

Please Don't Feed the Alligator

Daufuskie Freeze

This drink is named after a beautiful and untouched island near Hilton Head Island. The drink itself has become probably the most popular drink I serve at Hilton Head. It is seemingly a perfect combination of ingredients that compliment each other extremely well. Be careful, you too may also become a Daufuskie Island addict.

1 1/2 ounces light rum **1 1/2 ounces coconut cream**
2 ounces orange juice **3 - 4 medium strawberries**

Place strawberries, then ice into blender. Add remainder of ingredients and blend until smooth and creamy. One 12-ounce serving. Garnish with fresh strawberry.

Note: To prepare this drink using frozen strawberries, substitute 2 ounces of frozen strawberries for the fresh strawberries. Equally excellent without alcohol.

Pool Bar Jim's

Beachcomber's Gold

This drink has been one of my most pleasant surprises and has become the favorite of many who have tried it. With very few exceptions most customers who try this drink seldom switch to another. The drink is relatively simple, but the combination of these ingredients produces a most exotic drink. Once you try it, I think you'll agree.

1 1/2 ounces Grand Marnier   **1 ounce coconut cream**
2 ounces orange juice   **1/4 ounce orgeat syrup**

Place all ingredients in blender over ice selection. Select the proper blender speed and blend until consistently smooth. Garnish with orange wedge and cherry. One 12-ounce serving.

Pool Bar Jim's

Hilton Head Freeze

A great drink created as a tribute to a very elegant island. The drink is savory and delicious . . . the island is posh and beautiful.

1 1/2 ounces light rum   **1/2 ounce grenadine**
2 1/2 ounces orange juice   **1/2 ounce medium ripe**
1 1/2 ounces coconut cream   **banana**

Put banana in blender, add ice and remaining ingredients. Blend until creamy and stiff. One 12-ounce serving. Garnish with cherry. Equally excellent without alcohol.

Pool Bar Jim's

Hilton Head Island hosts the MCI Heritage Golf Classic at Harbour Town, and the Celebrity Golf Tournament at Palmetto Dunes among numerous other tournaments at its twelve championship golf courses. Shaped like a foot, the 42-square-mile island is divided into definable areas: the toe, the instep, the heel, and the ankle.

Flip

This refreshing drink was in vogue in England in the 18th century and was brought to Carolina when settled by the Lords Proprietors. The South Carolina Society of Colonial Dames owns a Flip bowl or glass. It is of glass, small at the bottom and gradually widens to the top. It holds about a quart.

4 jiggers whiskey   **1 quart rich milk**
4 egg yolks   **Nutmeg to taste**
4 teaspoons sugar

Beat yolks, sugar, and seasoning together. Add milk and whiskey. Shake well with crushed ice, strain and serve in stemmed glasses with a dash of nutmeg on top. Serves 8-10.

Charleston Receipts

Fiduciary Goonerizer

Another customer preference creation. The desire for "something different" can bring about some fantastic drink creations as well as unusual names. A group of insurance representatives helped with this concoction.

3 medium fresh strawberries   **1/2 ounce half-and-half**
1 1/2 ounces vodka   **1/4 ounce grenadine**
1 ounce amaretto   **1 ounce coconut cream**

Place strawberries, then ice, then the remainder of the ingredients in blender. Blend until thoroughly mixed, frozen and smooth. Garnish with fresh strawberry.

Note: To prepare this drink with frozen strawberries, substitute 2 ounces frozen strawberries for the fresh strawberries. Equally excellent without alcohol.

Pool Bar Jim's

Roseanna Banana Kabana

The honor for the creation of this drink goes to Ralph Neely, a former bartender at the Myrtle Beach Hilton. The addition of a banana to a Kahlua Frost proved a sensational creation. Originally called a Kabana, I felt it was deserving of a more appropriate name.

1 1/2 ounces Kahlua   **1 ounce half-and-half**
1 1/2 ounces coconut cream   **1/2 medium ripe banana**

Place banana in blender and add remaining ingredients. Blend until rich and creamy. Garnish with cherry. One 12-ounce serving.

Pool Bar Jim's

Easy Almond Amaretto Cream

Excellent on fruit.

1 cup sour cream
3 tablespoons confectioners'
  sugar

1/2 teaspoon almond extract
3 tablespoons amaretto
  liqueur

Mix all together. Use as a dip for fresh strawberries or on top of other fresh fruit. Yields 1 cup.

Charleston Receipts Repeats

Amaretto Cheese Spread

1 (8-ounce) package cream cheese

1/4 cup amaretto liqueur

1 (2 1/2-ounce) package slivered almonds, sautéed in butter

Soften cream cheese and blend in amaretto. Form a ball and chill until firm. Before serving, cover with almonds and allow to reach room temperature. Serve with thinly sliced apples and pears.

This also may be served as after-dinner fruit and cheese.

Putting On The Grits

Hot Artichoke Cheese

1 (8 1/2-ounce) can artichokes, drained, and cut in small bite-size pieces

1 cup Parmesan cheese

1 cup Hellman's mayonnaise

Mix together and bake in flat baking dish 20 minutes at 350° until brown on top.

Serve hot on crackers. Triple for large casserole. Hellman's mayonnaise is a must. This brand does not make the casserole greasy.

Carolina Cuisine Encore!

Beautiful Corinthian granite columns welcome you into the State House in Columbia. Bronze stars mark where shells from Sherman's army struck during the Civil War. It is recognized as "one of the notable buildings of the world."

Cheese Planks

4 slices bacon
4 ounces cheese, shredded
1 small onion, chopped
1 (2 1/2-ounce) package
  slivered almonds
1/2 cup mayonnaise

1 teaspoon Worcestershire
  sauce
Salt to taste
Pepper to taste
18 or more slices thin
  sliced white bread

Fry bacon until crisp. Put bacon, cheese, onion and almonds in food processor and chop until fine. Remove from processor and mix with mayonnaise, Worcestershire sauce, salt and pepper. Trim crust from bread slices and spread with cheese mixture. Slice each piece into 4 strips. Place on baking pan and bake at 350° for 15 minutes or until crisp. Yield: 24 servings.

Note: Can be made ahead and frozen.

Prescriptions for Good Eating

Cheese Bennes

1/2 pound sharp Cheddar
cheese, grated
1/4 pound margarine or
butter, softened
1/2 teaspoon salt

Pinch cayenne
1 1/4 cup sifted flour
1/2 cup benne seeds (sesame
seeds) roasted

Cream first four ingredients together. Add flour and knead. Add seeds and knead. Form into four or five long thin rolls. Chill in wax paper several hours or freeze.

Slice rolls into "thin dimes". Bake at 350° for 10-15 minutes. If desired, sprinkle with salt while hot. Keep in tightly covered tin. Makes: 10-12 dozen. Freezes well.

Charleston Receipts Repeats

Cheese Favors

1 stick margarine
1 cup grated sharp cheese
1 cup flour

1/8 teaspoon salt
2 tablespoons milk or cream
1 jar apple jelly

Cream margarine and cheese together. Add flour, salt, and milk, and mix well. Knead and roll on flour board. Cut with biscuit cutter. Add 1/4 teaspoon of apple jelly and fold over. Crimp edges. For variety, add dates and nuts to apple jelly or fig preserves as filling. Cook at 350° for 15 minutes. Yields 36.

Carolina Cuisine

The oldest landscaped garden in America is Middleton Gardens on the banks of the Ashley River near Charleston. Here the first camellias were introduced and butterfly lakes were constructed to reflect the sky and set off the magnificent brick plantation home.

Mincemeat Tea Sandwiches

1 (8-ounce) package cream
  cheese, softened
1/2 cup mayonnaise
1/2 cup finely chopped
  crystallized ginger

1/2 cup mincemeat
1/2 cup toasted pecans
2 loaves thin sliced bread,
  crust removed

Mix in medium bowl cream cheese, mayonnaise, ginger, mincemeat and pecans. Blend thoroughly. Spread on bread and
make sandwich. Cut in half, strips or triangles. Yield: 5 dozen.

Prescriptions for Good Eating

Bollin Party Sandwiches

1 (8-ounce) package cream
  cheese
1 (4 1/2-ounce) can pitted
  black olives, drained and
  sliced
6 - 7 slices crisp bacon,
  crumbled
1 cup finely chopped toasted
  pecans

1 cup chopped fresh parsley
1 small onion, grated
2 teaspoons lemon juice
Salt and pepper to taste
Mayonnaise for desired
  consistency
Sandwich bread

Soften cheese and add other ingredients. Mix well. Spread
filling generously to make sandwiches. Trim crusts and cut
into triangles. Yields 7 dozen small sandwiches.

Putting On The Grits

 The Spartanburg Phillies, a minor league team affiliated with the
Philadelphia Phillies, play in season at Duncan Park.

Parmesan Chicken Fingers

8 boneless chicken breast
  halves
2 cups dry bread crumbs
3/4 cup grated Parmesan
  cheese
1 teaspoon salt

1/2 teaspoon pepper
1/4 cup chopped fresh
  parsley
2 garlic cloves, chopped
1 cup butter, melted

Remove skin and cut each chicken breast into 3-4 fingers. In large bowl combine bread crumbs, cheese, salt, pepper and parsley. Sauté garlic in butter. Remove from heat; add chicken fingers and let sit for 3 minutes. Dip chicken in bread crumbs and place in a 9x12x2-inch baking dish. Top fingers with more bread crumbs and pour remaining butter over all. Bake at 400° for 18-20 minutes. Cool slightly and cover loosely with foil. Refrigerate until well-chilled and transport in cooler. Yield: 24 chicken fingers.

Uptown Down South

Party Ham Rolls

1 stick margarine
3 tablespoons prepared
  mustard
3 tablespoons poppy seed
1 teaspoon Worcestershire
  sauce

1 medium grated onion and
  juice
2 packages party rolls (24
  to a package)
1/2 pound sliced, boiled ham

Melt margarine; remove from heat and add next 4 ingredients. Keep warm.

Meanwhile slice rolls and cut slices of ham to size of roll. Spread rolls with mixture and top with ham. Makes 48.

Feeding the Faithful

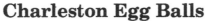

Charleston Egg Balls

8 hard boiled eggs, cooled
1/2 cup butter
1 teaspoon salt
1/4 teaspoon red pepper

1/2 teaspoon Worcestershire
sauce
1/4 teaspoon celery seed
1 cup bread crumbs

With a electric mixer or food processor, cream eggs and butter until well blended. Add salt, pepper, Worcestershire sauce and celery seed. Refrigerate several hours. Form mixture into 1-inch balls, then roll in bread crumbs. Makes 30 balls.

Since butter is used instead of mayonnaise, there is less chance of spoiling. This was important in the warm climate of Charleston prior to refrigeration and air conditioning. May be frozen.

One Course At A Time

Savory Eggs for Sandwiches

2 medium onions, chopped
1/2 bell pepper, chopped
1/2 stick butter or
   margarine
2 medium or 1 large ripe
   tomato, chopped
Sweet basil, not leaves but
   dried seed heads grown in
   your garden

Salt to taste
Pepper
Nature's seasoning
Celery salt
8 eggs, beaten
Grated cheese
Soy sauce (optional)

Sauté onions and peppers in margarine. Add tomato and basil and simmer until liquid is cooked away. Add remaining seasonings. Add beaten eggs to above mixture and cook over medium heat until done. Grated cheese or soy sauce may be added if desired. Let cool and add mayonnaise or salad dressing to spread well.

The Museum Cookbook

Vegetable Sandwich

1 large tomato
1 cucumber
1 green pepper

1/2 onion (small)
1 carrot

Grind all together. Drain and add:

1 teaspoon Worcestershire
   sauce
1 1/2 packages plain gelatin
   in 1/4 cup cold water,
   dissolved over hot water

1/2 teaspoon mustard
1 cup mayonnaise
1 1/2 teaspoons salt
1 teaspoon paprika

Mix all together and refrigerate. Sandwich spread will keep for several days.

Culinary Crinkles

Potato Skins

4 (2 - 2 1/2-pound) baked
  Russet potatoes
1/2 cup butter or margarine,
  melted
1 small clove garlic, minced

1/8 teaspoon paprika
Salt and pepper to taste
6 ounces Swiss cheese,
  sliced 1/8-inch thick
Chopped chives

Preheat oven to 450°. Quarter potatoes lengthwise. Carefully scoop pulp from skins, leaving 3/8 to 1/2-inch thick shell. Reserve pulp for other use.

Combine butter, garlic, paprika, salt, and pepper. Brush over inside of skins. Place skins on cookie sheet. Bake at 450° for 10 minutes or until crisp. Remove from oven. Top each with a slice of cheese and sprinkle with chives. Bake 2-3 minutes longer or until cheese melts. Yields 16 servings.

Per Serving: Calories 121, Protein 4 g, Fat 6 g, Cholesterol 18 mg,
  Fiber 1.2 g.
Percent of Calories: Protein 14%, Carbohydrates 43%, Fat 43%.

Palmetto Evenings

Vegetable Mold

1 package unflavored gelatin
1/4 cup cold water
1/4 cup boiling water
1 (3-ounce) package cream
  cheese
1 pint mayonnaise
1 tablespoon vinegar

Dash salt and pepper
1 small onion, chopped
2 tomatoes, chopped and
  drained
1 green pepper, chopped
1 peeled cucumber, chopped
1 cup chopped celery

Dissolve gelatin in cold water. Add boiling water and stir. Add cream cheese while hot and blend well. Cool and add mayonnaise, vinegar, salt, pepper, and vegetables. Refrigerate. This keeps a week or so and is good stuffed in tomatoes or spread on crackers and bread. Delicious.

Flavored With Tradition

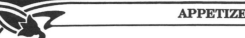

Marinated Mushrooms

I've never served these when someone hasn't asked for the recipe.

2 pounds mushrooms
3 quarts water
1 lemon
1/2 cup tarragon vinegar
3/4 cup oil
1 clove garlic, crushed
1 teaspoon salt

1/2 teaspoon freshly ground
   pepper
1 teaspoon basil
1 teaspoon oregano
1/4 cup chopped parsley
1 bay leaf

Prepare mushrooms by wiping clean and removing woody stem. In a large pot, bring water to a boil. Halve lemon, squeeze juice into water and toss in the rinds. Remove water from heat and add mushrooms. Blanch for 3 minutes. Drain. Mix together remaining ingredients and pour over mushrooms in a covered container. Refrigerate for 1-2 hours before serving. Drain and serve with toothpicks. Serves 24.

Calories 46.98, Protein 2.56gm, Fat 2.56gm, Carbohydrates 4.30gm, Fiber 0.76gm, Cholesterol 0.00mg, Saturated Fats 0.23gm, Iron 0.77mg, Calcium 6.30mg, Sodium 39.48mg, Potassium 393.80mg, Vitamin A 17.79I.U., Vitamin C 3.39mg, Thiamine 0.09mg, Riboflavin 0.44mg, Niacin 3.97mg.

The Enlightened Gourmet

Hot Crab and Cream Cheese Dip

8 ounces cream cheese,
softened
1 tablespoon half-and-half

8 ounces white crabmeat
2 tablespoons grated onion
1 teaspoon horseradish

Combine all ingredients and blend well in casserole dish. Bake at 350° for 12-15 minutes. Serve with toasted bread rounds. Serves 6-8.

Hudson's Cookbook

Shrimp-Cottage Cheese Dip

1/2 pound fresh cooked
shrimp
1 cup creamed cottage cheese
3 tablespoons chili sauce
1 teaspoon finely grated
onion

1 teaspoon lemon juice
1/2 teaspoon Worcestershire
sauce
2 - 3 tablespoons milk
1/2 - 1 teaspoon horseradish
(or to taste)

Chop cleaned shrimp very fine and combine with cottage cheese in bowl, using electric mixer on medium speed. (Can also be blended by hand.) Add seasonings, plus dash of salt. Blend to a creamy mixture on low speed. Chill.

Serve with pieces of fresh vegetables, potato chips, crackers, or whatever you have.

Stirrin' The Pots On Daufuskie

Crab or Caviar Mousse

1 package unflavored gelatin	1 teaspoon Worcestershire
1/2 cup water	1/2 teaspoon salt
1 cup sour cream	1/4 teaspoon cayenne pepper
1 cup mayonnaise	1 pound crab meat or
1 tablespoon grated onion	1/2 pound caviar
1 tablespoon lemon juice	

Dissolve the gelatin in the water and cool. Mix everything except crab meat or caviar together. Blend in crab meat or caviar carefully. Pour into a mold which has been greased with a little mayonnaise. Refrigerate to set. Unmold and serve with Melba toast.

Flavored With Tradition

Shrimp Mold

1/2 cup water	2 packages Good Season
1 package unflavored gelatin	Italian Dry Mix
4 teaspoons lemon juice	2 cups sour cream
1 (8-ounce) package cream	1 cup shrimp, chopped
cheese, softened	

Mix water with gelatin and let stand for a few minutes. Add lemon juice and heat until gelatin dissolves. Add all other ingredients. Mix and pour into greased mold. Refrigerate and serve with crackers.

Cooking on the Go

More than 500 years have passed since South Carolina's Grand Strand was first inhabited by the Waccamaw and Winyah Indians.

Super Chalupa

A real hit for Mexican food lovers and everyone else as well.

1 1/2 pounds ground beef
1 cup chopped onion
1 teaspoon salt
1/2 teaspoon pepper
1 tablespoon chili powder
1 (17-ounce) can refried beans
1 (7-ounce) can green chilies, diced, optional
4 cups grated Cheddar cheese

1 (7-ounce) can green chili salsa or 7-ounce bottle of green taco sauce
1 (8-ounce) carton sour cream
2 cups Guacamole Dip
3 bunches green onions, chopped
1 (4 1/2-ounce) can ripe olives, chopped

Brown meat in large skillet; drain. Add onion, salt, pepper, chili powder, refried beans and chilies. Mix well. Pat mixture into a greased 9x13-inch baking dish. Top with cheese. Sprinkle chili salsa or taco sauce over top. This may be prepared ahead of time and refrigerated until cooking time. Preheat oven to 400° and cook 25-30 minutes. Remove from oven and spread with sour cream. Then cover with Guacamole Dip. Sprinkle with onions and olives, decorating according to your whim. Serves 20-30.

GUACAMOLE DIP:
1 (8-ounce) carton sour cream
1 avocado, mashed
1 teaspoon lemon juice

1/2 teaspoon garlic salt, optional
1/4 teaspoon onion juice, optional

Combine the above ingredients and chill.

Calories 169.44, Protein 10.50gm, Fat 11.70gm, Carbohydrates 5.95gm, Fiber 0.52gm, Cholesterol 40.94mg, Saturated Fats 5.69gm, Iron 1.30mg, Calcium 143.94mg, Sodium 204.44mg, Potassium 249.23mg, Vitamin A 485.30 I.U., Vitamin C 2.94mg, Thiamine 0.06mg, Riboflavin 0.16mg, Niacin 1.34mg.

The Enlightened Gourmet

Crab Pie

This goes far because it is so rich.

1 pound backfin crab
1/2 bottle of capers
2 cups mayonnaise

1/2 cup grated sharp cheese
Crackers

Combine crab, capers, and mayonnaise. Put in pie plate and cover with grated cheese. Bake at 350° until cheese is melted, about 10 minutes. Serve hot on crackers. Yields 15 very generous servings.

Calories 254.66, Protein 6.55gm, Fat 25.30gm, Carbohydrates 0.88gm, Fiber 0.00gm, Cholesterol 54.73mg, Saturated Fats 4.83gm, Iron 0.43mg, Calcium 48.28mg, Sodium 266.62mg, Potassium 67.69mg, Vitamin A 790.74 I.U., Vitamin C 0.60mg, Thiamine 0.06mg, Riboflavin 0.05mg, Niacin 0.85mg

The Enlightened Gourmet

Chef Warren Snell's Oysters Rockefeller

1/2 pound spinach, washed
well and drained
6 scallions
1 stalk celery
1 clove garlic
1 cup butter
1/4 cup Parmesan cheese
1 cup of your favorite white
sauce

1 tablespoon Worcestershire
sauce
1/2 cup cooked diced bacon
1/2 teaspoon salt (if
desired)
Few dashes of Tabasco sauce
1 ounce Anisette
24 oysters, shucked

Finely chop the spinach, scallions, celery and garlic. Sauté in butter until soft. Melt the 1 cup butter then mix in the Parmesan cheese, white sauce, Worcestershire, bacon, salt, Tabasco and Anisette. Mix sauce with the vegetables.

Refrigerate mixture until ready to use. Spoon mixture onto the shucked oysters (enough to just cover). Set on pan and bake in preheated oven at 450° until hot, about 5 minutes. Top oysters with Bearnaise Sauce and serve immediately. From Fitzgerald's Restaurant.

Island Events Cookbook

Candied Peanuts

1 cup sugar   2 cups raw peanuts
1/2 cup water

Completely dissolve sugar in warm water, then add peanuts. Boil until it turns to sugar and all syrup evaporates. Be sure not to burn. Place on cookie sheet at 300° for 25 minutes. Stir occasionally.

Carolina Cuisine Encore!

Sugared Nuts

2 cups pecan halves   1 teaspoon cinnamon
1 cup sugar   1/2 teaspoon salt
5 tablespoons water   1 teaspoon vanilla

Toast nuts at 350° about 8 minutes. Cook other ingredients (except vanilla) until soft ball stage is reached (234°). Remove from heat and add vanilla. Add nuts and stir until sugar coats nuts and becomes sugary. The nuts will have a frosty appearance. Lift out and place on rack to cool. Separate.

Southern Cooking

South Carolina is known for its beautiful gardens. Among them are Middleton, Magnolia, Cypress, and White Point, all near Charleston; Brookgreen near Murrells Inlet; Glencairn in Rock Hill; Edisto in Orangeburg; Hopeland in Aiken; Kalmia in Hartsville; Wells Japanese Gardens in Newberry; Swan Lake Iris at Sumter; and Clemson Horticultural Gardens in Clemson.

Soups

A lovely, lacy footbridge at Magnolia Gardens reflects the beautiful spring
flowers in the black cypress lake waters.

She-Crab Soup

"She-crab" is much more of a delicacy than "he-crab," as the eggs add a special flavor to the soup. The street vendors make a point of calling "she-crab" loudly and of charging extra for them.

1 tablespoon butter	Few drops onion juice
1 teaspoon flour	1/8 teaspoon mace
1 quart milk	1/8 teaspoon pepper
2 cups white crabmeat and	1/2 teaspoon Worcestershire
crab eggs	4 tablespoons dry sherry
1/2 teaspoon salt	1/4 pint cream (whipped)

Melt butter in top of double boiler and blend with flour until smooth. Add the milk gradually, stirring constantly. To this add crabmeat and eggs and all seasonings except sherry. Cook slowly over hot water for 20 minutes. To serve, place one tablespoon of warmed sherry in individual soup bowls, then add soup and top with whipped cream. Sprinkle with paprika or finely chopped parsley. Secret: if unable to obtain "she-crabs," crumble yolk of hard boiled eggs in bottom of soup plates. Serves 4-6.

Charleston Receipts

Crab Stew

1/4 cup margarine	2 tablespoons flour
1/2 small onion, chopped	2 1/2 cups milk
1/2 stem celery, chopped	1/2 teaspoon salt
or 1/4 teaspoon celery seed	Dash pepper
1 cup fresh crabmeat or	
1 (6-ounce) can of crabmeat	

Melt margarine in heavy saucepan. Add chopped onion and celery and sauté until tender but not brown. Add crabmeat and stir for a minute or two. Sprinkle flour over crabmeat and stir well. Add milk and stir constantly until thickened. Season. Serve in bowls with crisp crackers. Serves 4.

Strictly For Boys

Tidalholm Seafood Chowder

1/2 stick of butter or margarine

1/4 cup diced oysters and liquid

1 cup small peeled raw shrimp

1 quart milk

1/2 cup crabmeat

1 small can water chestnuts, thinly sliced, and the liquid

1 can whole kernel corn and the liquid

1 cup cooked white potatoes, diced and liquid

1 1/2 cups cooked fish, diced (can be leftover baked fish)

Salt and pepper to taste

Parsley (optional)

1 pint half-and-half

Sauté oysters and shrimp in butter about 3-4 minutes. Add milk and turn heat low. Add next 7 ingredients and cook very slowly for 10 minutes. Stir often. Then add half-and-half and heat another minute very carefully stirring. (Too much heat will cause the half-and-half to separate). If freezing is desired, omit potatoes until serving time.

Variation: Add or delete seafoods as available.

Catch-of-the-Day

Creamy Oyster Broccoli Stew

3 cups milk
2 (11-ounce) cans condensed
   Cheddar cheese soup
1 (10-ounce) package frozen
   chopped broccoli
1 cup frozen loose-pack hash
   brown potatoes

1 small onion, chopped
1 tablespoon butter
1 pint shucked oysters or
   two (8-ounce) cans whole
   oysters

In 3-quart saucepan combine milk and soup. Stir in broccoli, potatoes, and onion. Cook, stirring occasionally, over medium heat until bubbly, breaking up broccoli with fork till thawed. Simmer, covered, for 10 minutes. Remove from heat; cool. Cover and chill. At serving time, in 3-quart saucepan reheat soup. In separate pan, sauté the fresh drained oysters in butter; cook over medium heat till edges curl. Add to broccoli mixture; heat through. (If using canned oysters, just add undrained oysters directly to soup; heat through.) Serves 4-6.

Island Events Cookbook

Oyster Stew

1/4 pound bacon thinly sliced
1 stick butter
1 cup chopped celery
1/2 cup chopped green onions
2 cups heavy cream

Pinch cayenne pepper
Pinch white pepper
Pinch salt
Tabasco and Worcestershire to taste
3 dozen oysters, save liquid

Cook bacon in pan until crisp. Drain off half the grease and discard. Add half the butter and sauté celery and green onions until barely cooked. Add heavy cream, cayenne pepper, white pepper, salt, Tabasco and Worcestershire. Bring to boil, shaking pan (rather than stirring) until cream thickens. Add oysters and their liquid and cook just until oyster edges curl. Ladle into cups (or bowls) distributing oysters evenly. Drop a small chunk of butter into each cup and garnish with a sprinkle of paprika and a pinch of parsley. Goes especially well at Christmas using the above colorful garnish.

Hudson's Cookbook

New England Clam Chowder

1 can cream of celery soup
2 cans cream of potato soup
2 cans minced or chopped clams
3 slices bacon, fried and crumbled (optional)

2 soup cans milk
1/2 small onion, minced
Dash of marjoram

Mix all the ingredients together, heat until piping hot and serve. Makes 4-6 servings.

Cooking on the Go

39

Seafood Gumbo

SHRIMP STOCK:

2 quarts water
1 1/2 pounds raw shrimp in
  shell
2 large onions, quartered,
  skin left on
3 stalks celery, cut in
  1-inch pieces

5 bay leaves
1 tablespoon thyme leaves
Juice of 2 lemons
2 teaspoons Hudson's
  Seasoning

Combine all ingredients in stockpot. Boil 15-20 minutes, or until onions and celery are transparent. Shrimp should be somewhat overcooked to extract the most flavor from them. Strain, reserving the liquid, then pick out the shrimp and peel. Chop shrimp in small pieces and reserve.

SOUP:

3 cloves chopped garlic
2 large onions, diced
1 bell pepper, largely diced
2 stalks celery, largely
  diced
1 stick butter
1 cup flour (browned or
  roasted)
Reserved shrimp stock
  from above
2 cups tomato concasse
  (method follows)*
Cayenne pepper to taste

Salt to taste
1 teaspoon thyme
3 teaspoons gumbo filé
  powder (if not
  available in your area.,
  soup is worth making
  even without it)
1 pint oysters
1/2 pound special (flake)
  crabmeat
Reserved chopped shrimp
  from stock

Sauté garlic, onions, peppers, and celery in butter until tender. Spread flour out in pan and bake in 350° oven until light brown. Add browned flour and cook 3 minutes over medium heat. Add stock a pint at a time, whisking after each addition. Add tomatoes and simmer 45 minutes, stirring occasionally. At this point soup should be thick enough to coat the back of a spoon; if not—simmer another 15 minutes. Add seasonings (except file powder), oysters, crabmeat, and shrimp.

CONTINUED

CONTINUED

Simmer 5 more minutes and take off heat. Combine filé powder with a little water then stir into soup (as you would treat cornstarch). Serve garnished with white steamed rice or potato salad.

*Tomatoes Concasse—Dip tomatoes in boiling water for 5 seconds. Peel off skin and squeeze out seeds and liquid. Dice remainder coarsely.

Hudson's Cookbook

Charleston Gumbo

Good on your rice the day there is no gravy.

2 slices of bacon	1/2 small onion chopped
1 pint can tomatoes	Salt, pepper and
1 quart okra	Worcestershire to taste

Broil bacon, add tomatoes, chopped okra and onion, salt, pepper and Worcestershire. Let simmer for two hours. Serves 6.

Charleston Receipts

Extra Good Vegetable Soup

3 medium onions, chopped	2 large cans tomatoes,
1 pound ground lean beef	chopped
1 cup diced potatoes	1 cup dry red burgundy wine
1 cup diced celery	2 tablespoons parsley
1 cup diced green beans	1/2 teaspoon basil
1 cup diced carrots	1/4 teaspoon thyme
3 cans beef consommé soup	1 cup water

Sauté onions. Cook ground meat until done and drain. Simmer onions, ground meat and all remaining ingredients for 1 1/2 hours. A crockpot or slow cooker works well for this soup. Makes 3 quarts.

Carolina Cuisine Encore!

Vegetable Cheddar Chowder

1/2 cup onion, chopped	1/4 cup all-purpose flour
1 clove garlic, pressed	2 cups milk
1 cup celery, sliced	1 tablespoon prepared
3/4 cup carrots, sliced	mustard
1 cup potatoes, peeled and	1/4 teaspoon white pepper
cubed	1/8 teaspoon paprika
3 1/2 cups chicken broth	2 tablespoons pimiento,
1 (17-ounce) can corn,	diced
drained	2 cups Cheddar cheese
1/4 cup butter or margarine	

In a Dutch oven, combine onion, garlic, celery, carrots, potatoes and chicken broth. Bring to a boil, cover and reduce heat. Simmer 15-20 minutes. Stir in corn and remove from heat. In a saucepan, melt butter over low heat. Add flour and stir until smooth. Cook 1 minute. Gradually add milk. Cook over medium heat, stirring constantly, until thick and bubbly. Stir in remaining ingredients. Cook until cheese melts. Gradually add cheese mixture to vegetables. Cook over medium heat until chowder is thoroughly heated. Yields 2 quarts and serves 6-8. Best when made a day ahead.

Stir Crazy!

Quick Onion Soup

1/8 pound butter	1 cup grated Swiss or
3 large onions, sliced thin	Parmesan cheese
3 cans consommé	1 cup croutons
1/4 cup red wine	

Melt butter and sauté onions until clear. Add consommé and wine. Pour into oven casserole, sprinkle with cheese and bake in a preheated 350° oven for 30 minutes. To brown the cheese, broil for a minute after cooking. Pass the croutons. Serves 4.

Cooking on the Go

Broccoli - Cream Cheese Soup

1 cup chopped green onion
4 tablespoons butter
32 ounces cream cheese
4 cups half-and-half
4 cups chicken broth
6 (10-ounce) packages frozen
  chopped broccoli

2 teaspoons lemon juice
2 teaspoons salt
1 teaspoon pepper
Slivered almonds
Fresh parsley

Sauté green onions in butter in large saucepan or Dutch oven. Cube cream cheese. Add cubed cheese and cream to onions and stir over low heat until cheese is melted. Stir in chicken broth; set aside. Cook broccoli according to package directions and drain. Blend half of broccoli mixture in food processor or blender until smooth. Add processed broccoli and remaining chopped broccoli to soup mixture. Stir in lemon juice and seasonings. Heat thoroughly. Toast almonds and serve with a sprig of parsley. Serves 16.

Uptown Down South

Potato Cheese Soup

3 medium potatoes
2 cups boiling water
3 cups milk
2 tablespoons butter or
  margarine
1 small onion (finely
  chopped)

2 tablespoons flour
1 teaspoon salt
1/4 teaspoon cayenne
1 cup grated Cheddar cheese

Cook potatoes in boiling water. Drain almost all of the water out and mash the potatoes coarsely. Add milk and heat to a simmer. Melt butter, add onion and simmer until onion is transparent. Add flour and seasonings. Combine with potato mixture and simmer, stirring every 5 minutes. Add cheese and beat until smooth. Serve hot, garnished with chives and crushed potato chips. Serves 4.

The Sandlapper Cookbook

Cabbage Soup

1 head savoy cabbage,
  shredded
3 onions, sliced
1 green pepper, chopped fine
Bouquet garni—tied
  securely (bay leaf, 6 sprigs
  parsley, sprig of thyme) in
  cheesecloth

3 cups milk
1 cup sour cream
2 tablespoons butter
2 tablespoons flour
Grated Swiss cheese
Crisp bacon bits, optional
Salt and pepper, to taste

Cover "veggies" and bouquet garni with cold water and cook until cabbage is done, onions very soft and liquid is reduced by 1/2. Discard seasoning bag. Scald milk and sour cream separately, then combine with cabbage mixture. Cream butter and flour and stir into soup. Don't let it come to a boil again! Serve with grated Swiss cheese and bacon bits.

Bethel Food Bazaar II

Cold Peach Soup

3 cups sliced canned peaches
1 cup sour cream or vanilla
  yogurt

1/4 teaspoon almond extract

Blend ingredients in blender. Chill before serving and garnish with a fresh strawberry and/or sprig of mint. I like to serve this soup as an appetizer with Mexican and other highly seasoned foods. It's good on a hot summer day!

The Museum Cookbook

 South Carolina is first in peach production for the fresh market. Gaffney hosts the July Peach Festival. An eye-catching sight there is the *peachoid*, a one-million-gallon water tank shaped like a peach.

Cold Zucchini Soup

4 medium zucchini, unpeeled	4 strips bacon
5 medium new potatoes, unpeeled	Sour cream
	Croutons
1 medium onion	Crumbled bacon
1 can beef consommé	

Slice zucchini, potatoes and onion and boil until tender. Drain and put one-third of cooked ingredients in blender with 1/3 can of consommé. Blend remainder the same way. Chill thoroughly. Before serving blend a heaping teaspoon of sour cream into each serving. Garnish with croutons and crumbled bacon. Serves 8.

Flavored With Tradition

Frosty Tomato Cream

Wonderful!

1 small onion, peeled and
  chopped
1 small cucumber, peeled and
  chopped
8 sprigs parsley

1 cup yogurt or sour cream
1 (10 3/4-ounce) can tomato
  soup
1 (10 3/4-ounce) can chicken
  broth

In a blender, purée onion, cucumber, and parsley. Blend in yogurt or sour cream and tomato soup. Skim fat from broth and blend broth with other ingredients. Chill. Approximate yield: 6 (2/3 cup) servings.

Calories 74.98, Protein 3.95gm, Fat 1.79gm, Carbohydrates 11.60gm, Fiber 0.41gm, Cholesterol 9.48mg, Saturated Fats 0.50gm, Iron 1.04mg, Calcium 67.74mg, Sodium 715.63mg, Potassium 281.36mg, Vitamin A 535.49 I.U., Vitamin C 12.14mg, Thiamine 0.5mg, Riboflavin 0.11mg, Niacin 1.09mg

The Enlightened Gourmet

Cold Tomato Soup

3 cups tomato juice
2 tablespoons tomato paste
  or chopped tomatoes
4 tablespoons scallions,
  chopped
2 tablespoons lemon juice

1/2 teaspoon curry powder
1/2 lemon rind, grated
Salt and pepper to taste
Thyme to taste
1 cup sour cream
Sugar

Mix first 8 ingredients. Chill. Before serving, add sugar to taste and sour cream, well blended. Serves 4-6.

Sea Island Seasons

Salads

Sea Pines Plantation. Hilton Head Island.

Congealed Cranberry Salad

2 (3-ounce) packages lemon
  gelatin
1 (16-ounce) can whole berry
  cranberry sauce
2 cups boiling water
1 (8 1/4-ounce) can crushed
  pineapple, drained and
  liquid reserved

1/2 - 1 cup celery, finely
  chopped
Mayonnaise
Nutmeg

Dissolve gelatin and cranberry sauce in boiling water. Add pineapple. When gelatin begins to jell, add celery. Serve topped with mayonnaise which has been softened with reserved pineapple juice. Sprinkle with ground nutmeg. Serves 8.

Sea Island Seasons

Congealed Orange Jello Salad

2 (3-ounce) boxes orange
  gelatin
2 cups boiling water
2 (11-ounce) cans mandarin
  oranges, drained

1 (6-ounce) can frozen
  orange juice
1 (8 1/4-ounce) can crushed
  pineapple, undrained

Combine ingredients thoroughly and pour into a 9x13-inch pan. Chill until set.

TOPPING:
1 (3-ounce) box lemon
  instant pudding
1 cup milk

1 envelope Dream Whip or 1
  small carton Cool Whip

Mix pudding with 1 cup milk. Mix Dream Whip according to directions. Combine pudding and Dream Whip and spread on salad. Serves 8-12. Looks quite sweet, but it is not!

Carolina Cuisine Encore!

Easy Strawberry Salad

1 large strawberry Jello
1 envelope plain gelatin
2 cups boiling water
1 large package frozen
    strawberries
1 large can crushed
    pineapple, drained

1 cup chopped nuts
1/2 (6-ounce) package small
    marshmallows
1 cup sour cream
1 large cream cheese
1/2 cup sugar

Combine dry Jello and plain gelatin. Add 2 cups boiling water and stir well. Add strawberries, drained pineapple, nuts, and marshmallows. Pour into long casserole and congeal. Mix sour cream, cream cheese and sugar with mixer. Spread on top of salad; chill.

Seasoned with Light

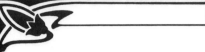

Cherry Sherry Salad

1 (6-ounce) package cherry
gelatin
1 1/3 cups boiling water
1 (16 1/2-ounce) can pitted
dark cherries, juice
reserved

1/4 - 1/2 cup dry sherry
1 1/2 cups seedless grapes
1 cup chopped pecans

Dissolve gelatin in boiling water. Add cold water to reserved
cherry juice to make 1 3/4 cups liquid and add to gelatin. Stir
in sherry. Refrigerate until slightly thickened. Cut grapes
and cherries in half. Place fruit and pecans in oiled 6-cup salad
mold or individual molds. Add gelatin mixture and chill until
firm. Unmold and serve with mayonnaise. Serves 8-10.
Canned pears may be substituted for grapes.

Putting On The Grits

Grapefruit Salad

1 (No. 2) can grapefruit
(2 1/2 cups)
1 (No 2) can white cherries
(seeded) (2 1/2 cups)
1 (No. 2) can sliced
pineapple (2 1/2 cups)
2 envelopes gelatine
dissolved in 1/2 cup of
cold water

1 lemon (juice)
1 cup almonds (blanched and
chopped coarsely)
Salt

Drain off all juices and let them come to boil. Add gelatine
and juice of one lemon, add fruit and almonds. Salt to taste.
Pour into molds and let harden. Serve on lettuce with mayonnaise. Serves 6.

Charleston Receipts

Blueberry Salad

1 large can crushed
  pineapple, drained, save
  juice
1 package (large) black
  cherry or blackberry Jello

1 cup cold water
1 can blueberry pie filling

Add enough water to pineapple juice to make 2 cups. Bring to a boil and add to gelatin. Stir until dissolved. Add 1 cup of cold water. Add pineapple and blueberry pie filling and let congeal. Cover with Topping:

1 large package cream cheese
1/2 cup sour cream

1/2 cup sugar
1 cup chopped nuts

Mix together and spread over congealed gelatin mixture.

Feeding the Faithful

Amazing Grace Salad

1 can Eagle Brand sweetened
  condensed milk
3 tablespoons lemon juice
1 large carton Cool Whip

1 large can crushed
  pineapple, drained
1 cup chopped nuts

Mix all ingredients together for a good salad. Set in refrigerator prior to serving. Serves 6-8. Delicious.

Variation: For Cherry Pineapple Salad, omit lemon juice and nuts. Add 1 banana and use 1 medium can pineapple and 1 medium carton Cool Whip. Add 1 can cherry pie filling. Pour into a pan and freeze.

A Taste of South Carolina

Charleston is often called the Holy City, for her skyline is punctuated with the graceful spires of lovely and historic churches. Within the city, there are 181 churches of 25 denominations.

Fruit Salad Strata

2 cups shredded lettuce
2 cups peaches, peeled and
  sliced*
2 cups strawberries
2 cups bananas, sliced*
1 cup flavored yogurt
1/2 cup shredded Swiss
  cheese

Place half of the lettuce in bottom of large glass bowl. Top with layer of peaches, then layer of strawberries, then layer of bananas. Sprinkle remaining lettuce. Spread yogurt over top; sprinkle with shredded cheese. Cover and chill for several hours. Gently toss to serve. Makes 12 servings.
   *Use lemon juice to prevent browning.

The Peach Sampler

Cranberry Waldorf Salad

2 cups raw cranberries
3 cups marshmallows
3/4 cup sugar
2 cups diced unpared tart
  apple
1/2 cup seedless green grapes
1/2 cup broken California
  walnuts
1/4 teaspoon salt
1 cup whipped cream

Grind cranberries and combine with marshmallows and sugar. Cover and chill overnight. Add apple, grapes, walnuts and salt. Fold in whipped cream. Chill. Serve in large bowl or individual lettuce cups. Garnish with clusters of grapes if desired. Serves 8-10.

Carolina Cuisine

Buttermilk Salad

2 small packages strawberry
  Jello
1 large can crushed
  pineapple

2 cups buttermilk
1 large Cool Whip

Bring the first 2 ingredients to a boil. Remove from heat and cool. Mix together the buttermilk and Cool Whip and add to the first mixture. Chill until firm.

500 Favorite Recipes

Hilton Head's small horses, known as "marsh tackies" or "Little horses of the march" are descendants of 89 purebred Arabian horses abandoned in Port Royal by a Spanish conquistador in the 16th century.

Broccoli-Cauliflower Salad

1 head broccoli florets
1 head cauliflower florets
1 can sliced water chestnuts
2 stalks chopped celery
1 small jar sliced mushrooms
1 small can sliced black olives
1 small bottle Kraft Italian dressing

Combine all ingredients in a large bowl. Pour Italian dressing over and stir well. Allow to marinate in refrigerator for 2 hours before serving.

Bethel Food Bazaar II

Autumn Tossed Salad

A refreshing change from the usual mixed vegetable tossed salad.

1/2 cup Good Seasons Italian Dressing, prepared
2 ounces bleu cheese, or more if desired
1 head lettuce, broken into bite-sized pieces
3 tart apples, cored and sliced into wedges (do not peel)
1 small red onion, sliced into rings

In large salad bowl, pour 1/4 cup salad dressing and add half of the bleu cheese. Mash the cheese into the dressing; blend until smooth. Add lettuce, apple slices, and onions. Crumble remaining bleu cheese on top. At serving time, toss well with remaining salad dressing. Add more dressing if desired. Serves 8.

Calories 153.21, Protein 2.57gm, Fat 11.21gm, Carbohydrates 12.72gm, Fiber 0.81gm, Cholesterol 6.09mg, Saturated Fats 2.73gm, Iron 0.68mg, Calcium 46.15mg, Sodium 365.08mg, Potassium 225.75mg, Vitamin A 350.85 I.U., Vitamin C 8.39mg, Thiamine 0.07mg, Riboflavin 0.10mg, Niacin 0.39mg

The Enlightened Gourmet

Korean Salad

SALAD:

1/2 pound spinach
1/2 head Romaine lettuce
3 hard-boiled eggs, grated
8 slices bacon, fried

1 (16-ounce) can bean
sprouts, drained
1 (8-ounce) can sliced water
chestnuts, drained

DRESSING:

1/2 cup vegetable oil
1/4 cup vinegar
1/3 cup ketchup
1/2 - 3/4 cup sugar

1 teaspoon Worcestershire
sauce
1 onion, grated
Salt and pepper to taste

Lightly toss greens with eggs and bacon. Combine dressing ingredients in a blender, and mix well. Immediately before serving, add bean sprouts and water chestnuts to salad. Pour dressing over salad, and toss lightly. Serves 8.

Stir Crazy!

Gourmet Chicken Salad with Fresh Peaches

A delicious luncheon main course.

2 cups chicken, cooked and
cubed
3/4 cup celery
3/4 cup white seedless
grapes
3/4 cup fresh peeled and
cubed peaches

1/2 cup mayonnaise
1/2 cup sour cream
Seasoning salt to taste
Fresh peach slices
Parsley

Lightly toss chicken, celery, grapes and peaches together. Mix mayonnaise and sour cream and pour over salad. Add seasoning salt and mix gently. Store in refrigerator until ready to use. Garnish with fresh peach slices and parsley. Makes 6 servings.

The Peach Sampler

Shell Point Shrimp Pasta Salad

1 pound shrimp, cooled, shelled and deveined
8 ounces sea shell pasta, boiled al dente
2 tablespoons olive oil
1 avocado, cubed and sprinkled with lime juice
1/2 cup chopped celery
1/2 cup chopped onion
1/2 cup chopped bell pepper
2 boiled eggs, chopped
1 cup shredded Cheddar cheese
1 teaspoon oregano
2 tablespoons parsley
1/8 teaspoon black pepper
1 teaspoon salt, or to taste
1/3 cup mayonnaise, or to taste
Paprika

Boil shrimp in salted water. Shell and devein. Boil pasta in salted water with 2 tablespoons olive oil. Cool and drain shrimp and pasta. Chop avocado and sprinkle with lime juice in large bowl. Chop celery, onion, bell pepper, and boiled eggs; add to avocado. Add shredded cheese. Add oregano, parsley, black pepper, and salt; toss gently. Add cool shrimp and pasta. Stir in mayonnaise. Sprinkle with paprika. Serve on lettuce leaf with Triscuits or sesame wafers on the side.

The Sandlappers' Salvation Cookbook

Hot Shrimp Salad with Pecans

1 cup boiled shrimp, chopped
1 cup celery, diced
1/4 cup mayonnaise
1/2 cup sharp cheese, grated
1/2 teaspoon onion juice
1 teaspoon lemon juice
1/2 cup pecans, crushed

Mix ingredients, except pecans, and place in casserole dish. Cover with crushed pecans and bake 30 minutes at 350°. Serves 4.

Southern Fish and Seafood Cookbook

Avocado Shrimp Salad

2 ripe avocados, peeled and halved
Lemon juice
1 pound raw, headless, peeled shrimp
1 small can pineapple rings (drained and minced)
1/2 cup bell pepper, finely chopped
1/2 cup celery, destringed and finely chopped
2/3 cup firm sour cream
1 teaspoon onion salt
1 cup Swiss cheese, shredded
Red tip lettuce, picked, washed and drained, for garnish

Coat avocado halves with lemon juice and chill. Cook shrimp in large quantity salted water for 3 minutes. Drain and cool in refrigerator. Combine pineapple, bell pepper, celery, sour cream, onion salt and shrimp. Refrigerate for 30-45 minutes. Scoop out hollow of avocado to allow room for mixture. Mound mixture on halves and cover with shredded cheese. Refrigerate until ready to serve. Serve on bed of lettuce.

Charleston Receipts Repeats

Shrimp Salad - Congealed

2 tablespoons plain gelatin
1/2 cup cold water
2 cups tomato juice
1 cup diced shrimp
10 stuffed olives, sliced
1 cup chopped celery
2 hard boiled eggs
Juice of 1 lemon
Salt, pepper, Tabasco, and Worcestershire

Dissolve gelatin in cold water. Stir into tomato juice. Put shrimp and other ingredients into molds. Season tomato juice well with lemon juice, salt, pepper, Tabasco and Worcestershire sauce. Pour into molds. Will make 8 large or 10 small servings.

DRESSING FOR SALAD:
1 cup mayonnaise
2 tablespoons grated cheese
2 tablespoons chili sauce

Culinary Crinkles

Summer Rice Salad

This can make an excellent summer lunch or supper.

**1 (6 1/2-ounce) jar marinated
  artichoke hearts**
1/3 cup mayonnaise
1 box Chicken Rice-a-Roni

1/4 teaspoon curry powder
1/2 cup chopped green pepper
6 spring onions, chopped

Remove artichokes from jar; add mayonnaise to remaining
marinade in jar. Cook Rice-a-Roni as directed; mix rest of
ingredients and combine with the rice. Refrigerate. To make
a complete meal platter, serve surrounded with hard-cooked
egg halves, sliced tomatoes, asparagus spears rolled in ham
slices, and black olives. Serves 6-8. This salad does not double
well.

Calories 163.20, Protein 2.40gm, Fat 8.00gm, Carbohydrates 20.61gm, Fiber
0.41gm, Cholesterol 14.37mg, Saturated Fats 1.39gm, Iron 0.84mg, Calcium 18.77mg, Sodium 660.75mg, Potassium 97.17mg, Vitamin A 68.25
I.U,.Vitamin C 15.62mg, Thiamine 0.09mg, Riboflavin 0.03mg, Niacin 0.79mg

The Enlightened Gourmet

Antipasta Salad

1 medium zucchini, thinly sliced
1 cup cauliflower flowerets
1 green onion, sliced
3/4 cup commercial Italian salad dressing
6 slices salami (6 ounces)
1 cup (4-ounces) cubed Provolone cheese
2 medium tomatoes cut in wedges
1 ripe avocado, peeled and sliced
1 small head leaf lettuce, torn
1 tablespoon grated Parmesan cheese

Combine zucchini, cauliflower and onion in a shallow container. Pour salad dressing over and toss lightly. Cover and chill 4 hours. Combine vegetables and next 5 ingredients in large bowl. Toss gently and sprinkle with Parmesan cheese.

Cooking...Done the Baptist Way

Potato Salad

10 medium potatoes
4 eggs
3 tablespoons salad relish
1 small jar diced pimento
1 small jar mushroom bits
2 ribs celery, chopped
1 medium bell pepper, chopped
1/2 cup water chestnuts, chopped
1 cup mayonnaise
1/4 cup mustard
1 teaspoon chili powder
Paprika
6 - 8 olives, sliced (to garnish)

Boil and cube potatoes and eggs. Chill. Mix all other ingredients except paprika and olives, then mix with potatoes and eggs. Put in clear glass or plastic bowl lined with lettuce leaves. Garnish with paprika and sliced olives. Yield: 12 servings. My family loves my potato salad!

Per Serving: Calories 235; Protein 4 g; Cholesterol 102; Fiber 1 g
Percent of Calories: Protein 6%; Carbohydrates 30%; Fat 64%

Palmetto Evenings

Tomato Aspic with Cream Cheese

2 tablespoons gelatin
1/4 cup cold water
1 can tomato soup
2 (3-ounce) cakes cream
  cheese
1 cup chopped celery
1 large (7 3/4-ounce) bottle
  stuffed olives (sliced)

1/4 teaspoon Worcestershire
  sauce
1/4 teaspoon black pepper
2 tablespoons tarragon
  vinegar

Dissolve gelatin in 1/4 cup cold water. Heat soup to boiling point, add cream cheese and stir until dissolved. Add gelatin and let stand until begins to congeal. Add other ingredients and pour in wet individual molds. Let stand in refrigerator overnight. One cup finely chopped nuts may be added. Serves 8.

The South Carolina Cook Book

Jamye's Tomato Aspic

3 (16-ounce) cans stewed
  tomatoes
3 envelopes unflavored
  gelatin
1 (8-ounce) can water
  chestnuts, drained and
  chopped

1 (3-ounce) jar
  pimiento-stuffed olives,
  drained and chopped
1 (14-ounce) can artichoke
  hearts, drained and
  quartered
1 teaspoon onion salt

Purée tomatoes in blender or food processor. Dissolve gelatin in 3/4 cup of tomato mixture. Heat remaining mixture until simmering. Remove from heat and add water chestnuts, olives, artichokes, onion salt and dissolved gelatin mixture. Chill in oiled individual molds until firm. Unmold, serve on lettuce and top with homemade mayonnaise. Serves 12.

Putting On The Grits

Bean Salad

1 cup oil	2 teaspoons salt
1 1/2 cups vinegar	1/2 teaspoon pepper
2 cups sugar	

Heat to boil. Cool, then pour over the following:

1 can green beans	1 can peas
1 can yellow beans	2 small onions (sliced)
1 can kidney beans	2 medium peppers (sliced)
1 can lima beans	

Mix well. Can be refrigerated for several weeks.

500 Favorite Recipes

Cucumber Mousse

2 (3-ounce) packages lime Jello dissolved in 1 1/2 cups hot water	1 onion, grated
	2 cups mayonnaise
2 medium cucumbers, unpeeled, grated and drained	1 pint cottage cheese
	1 teaspoon lemon juice
	3/4 cup slivered almonds

Mix together, pour in mold and let set. Serve on lettuce with tomato wedges and Poppy Seed Dressing.

POPPY SEED DRESSING:

1 cup salad oil	3 teaspoons mustard
1 cup salad dressing	2 tablespoons poppy seeds
1/3 cup vinegar	1 cup sugar

Mix well and keep refrigerated. (Keeps for weeks).

Cooking...Done the Baptist Way

 In the 1880's the textile industry began to flourish in the state. Today South Carolina is a leader in this industry.

Dot's Cole Slaw

A Pawley's Island favorite.

1 head cabbage	2 teaspoons sugar (to
1 onion (optional)	taste)
1 - 3 stalks celery	1 teaspoon salt (to taste)
1 cup mayonnaise	Pepper (optional)
2 tablespoons cider vinegar	Poppy seeds (optional)

Chop or grate cabbage, onion and celery. Combine remaining dressing ingredients. Mix with slaw. Chill several hours before serving to allow flavors to blend.

Catch-of-the-Day

Seven Day Slaw

This slaw is called 'Seven Day Slaw' because without any mayonnaise it will easily last for seven days.

1 head cabbage	2 tablespoons sugar
2 red onions	1/2 tablespoon dry mustard
1/3 cup sugar	1/4 tablespoon salt
1 cup oil	1/4 tablespoon black pepper
1 cup vinegar	

Slice cabbage and onions thinly or shred them. Toss with 1/3 cup of sugar. Mix remaining ingredients and bring to a boil. Pour boiling mixture over cabbage, let set, and in five minutes, mix. Chill in refrigerator and serve on leaves of romaine. Serves 4.

Hudson's Cookbook

 Cotton is king in Bishopville every October when the town hosts the Lee County Cotton Pickin' Festival.

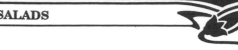

The Chart House's Bleu Cheese Dressing

3/4 cup sour cream
1/2 teaspoon dry mustard
1/2 teaspoon black pepper
1/2 teaspoon salt
1/3 teaspoon garlic powder

1 teaspoon Worcestershire
  sauce
1 1/3 cups mayonnaise
1/2 cup Danish bleu cheese

In a medium mixing bowl, combine sour cream, mustard, pepper, salt, garlic powder and Worcestershire sauce. Beat with an electric mixer for 2 minutes at low speed. Add mayonnaise, and blend for 30 seconds at low speed. Turn mixer to medium speed and blend for 2 more minutes. Crumble bleu cheese into small pieces and add to mixture. Blend at low speed 2-3 minutes. Chill in refrigerator for 24 hours before serving. Yields 2 1/2 cups.

South Carolina's Historic Restaurants

Hudson's House Dressing

1/2 quart mayonnaise	1/2 ounce lemon juice
2 dashes Tabasco	1/8 teaspoon garlic powder
3 tablespoons crushed black pepper	1/4 cup water
1/4 cup Parmesan cheese, grated	2 dashes Lea & Perrin

Mix all ingredients well and serve over a tossed green salad. Top with croutons. Yield: Approximately 3/4 quart.

Hudson's Cookbook

Roquefort Dressing

8 ounces Roquefort or bleu cheese, crumbled	1 small onion, grated
1 cup mayonnaise	1 tablespoon sugar
1/3 cup sour cream	Dash garlic powder
1 tablespoon cider vinegar, or a little more	Dash salt

Mix together well and refrigerate for a few hours. Can be used as a dip. If too thick, add a few drops of milk.

A Taste of South Carolina

House Dressing from Steak House Tavern

1 cup sugar	4 teaspoons Worcestershire sauce
3/4 cup red wine vinegar	1 clove garlic, minced
1 teaspoon dry mustard	1 1/2 cups salad oil
1 teaspoon paprika	
1/2 teaspoon salt	
1 (10 1/2-ounce) can tomato soup	

Beat all ingredients together until well blended. Chill overnight and shake well before serving.

Please Don't Feed the Alligators

Bread
and
Breakfast

Using palmetto fronds, march reeds, and other coastal region products,
Lowcountry natives weave beautiful baskets, an art that has been
passed down from generation to generation.

Southern Popovers

1 1/2 cups all-purpose flour   3 eggs, slightly beaten
1 1/2 cups milk   1/2 teaspoon salt

Combine all ingredients in blender and blend until smooth. Place well-buttered muffin tins in oven at 450° for 3 minutes or until a drop of water sizzles when dropped in them. Remove tins from oven; fill two-third's full with batter. Bake at 450° for 30 minutes; reduce heat to 300° and bake an additional 10-15 minutes. Serve immediately. Yields 1 dozen.

A Taste of South Carolina

Mom's Egg Bread

1 1/2 cups scalded milk,   1/2 cup Wesson oil
  cooled   1 tablespoon salt
3 eggs, beaten   3/4 cup sugar
2 packages dry yeast in 1/2   7 1/2 cups flour
  cup warm water

Mix and let rise. Work down and divide into 6 portions. Roll into rope type to braid, three portions to a loaf. Makes 2 loaves. Braid and put on a greased cookie sheet. Let rise again to double and 1/2 hour before baking, brush with 1 beaten egg and 1/4 cup water, mixed together. Sprinkle with sesame seeds. Bake at 350° till golden brown. Brush with butter.

500 Favorite Recipes

Farmers Hall Tea Room's
Sour Cream Biscuits

2 cups self-rising flour   2/3 cup sour cream
4 tablespoons shortening   1/2 - 3/4 cup milk

Mix flour, shortening and sour cream together. Add milk until mixture is thick enough to cling to a spoon. Drop by tablespoonful onto a greased pan. Bake in 450° oven for 8-10 minutes. Serve immediately. Yields 2 dozen.

South Carolina's Historic Restaurants

Sweet Potato Biscuits

3 cups flour
2 heaping tablespoons
  baking powder
1 teaspoon salt
1 cup vegetable shortening

2 cups mashed cooked sweet
  potatoes
1/2 cup sugar
1/4 cup milk

Sift together flour, baking powder and salt. Cut in shortening with fork or pastry cutter. Combine warm sweet potatoes and sugar, mixing well. Add milk. Combine sweet potato and flour mixtures. Blend well. Place on floured surface and roll to desired thickness or about 1/2 inch. Cut with biscuit cutter. Bake on lightly greased baking sheet at 400° for 10 minutes. Yields 2-3 dozen.

Great with pork, country ham or smoked turkey.

Putting On The Grits

Cream Cheese Biscuits

1 (3-ounce) package cream
  cheese
1 stick butter

1 cup all-purpose flour
1/2 teaspoon salt

Soften cream cheese and butter. Mix all ingredients and roll out to 1/4-inch or less thickness. Cut with small cookie cutter. Place on ungreased baking sheet and bake at 350° for 20 minutes or 400° for 10 minutes. Makes about 40 small biscuits.

Flavored With Tradition

Praline Biscuits

1/2 cup butter
1/2 cup packed brown sugar
36 pecan or walnut halves
Ground cinnamon

2 cups Bisquick baking mix
1/3 cup applesauce
1/3 cup milk

Place 2 teaspoons butter, 2 teaspoons brown sugar and 3 pecan halves in each of 12 muffin cups (2 1/2 x 1 1/4). Sprinkle cinnamon in each cup; heat in oven until melted. Mix baking mix, applesauce and milk until dough forms; beat 20 strokes. Spoon onto mixture in cups. Bake 10 minutes in a 450° preheated oven. Invert on heat-proof serving plate. Makes 12 biscuits.

Cooking...Done the Baptist Way

Caramel Nut Ring

1/2 cup butter
1/2 cup chopped pecans
1 cup brown sugar, firmly
  packed

2 tablespoons water
2 (8-ounce) cans crescent
  dinner rolls

Melt butter in small saucepan. Use 2 tablespoons to coat bottom and sides of 12-cup Bundt pan. Sprinkle pan with 3 tablespoons of chopped pecans. Add remaining nuts, brown sugar, and water to remaining butter. Heat to a boil, stirring occasionally. Remove dinner rolls from can but do not unroll. Cut each can of rolls into 16 slices, cut side up, in bottom of pan, overlapping slices. Separate each slice slightly to allow sauce to penetrate. Spoon half the caramel nut sauce over slices. Repeat next layer with second can of rolls and top with remaining caramel sauce. Bake at 350° for 25-30 minutes or until golden brown. Cool 3 minutes. Turn onto serving platter and slice. Freezes well. Serves 8-10.

Uptown Down South

Stickies

DOUGH:

1 yeast cake
1/2 cup warm water
1/2 cup shortening
1/4 cup sugar

1/2 cup boiling water
1 egg
3 1/2 cups self-rising flour

Dissolve yeast cake in 1/2 cup warm water. Cream shortening and sugar and 1/2 cup boiling water. Whip egg and add to dissolved yeast cake. Mix the above ingredients and add to flour. Put in another bowl greased with oleo. Cover and chill in refrigerator. This can be used successfully in a few hours or kept overnight. It takes about 1/2 cup flour to roll dough to 1/8-inch thickness. Use small biscuit cutter—makes 90.

TOPPING:

3 mellow apples
1 cup sugar
1/4 cup brown sugar

1 teaspoon cinnamon
1 stick of melted butter
Powdered sugar

Slice rather mellow apple in thin pieces and put in center of stickies. Heavily sprinkle apple slices with sugar mixture—1 cup sugar, 1/4 cup brown sugar with 1 teaspoon cinnamon. Drip a few drops of melted butter with brush. Bake on greased cookie sheet at 400° for 15 minutes. Dust with powdered sugar when ready to serve.

This recipe can be used for dinner rolls. Roll the dough to 1/8-inch thickness, and fold as for Parker House rolls.

"Don't Forget the Parsley. . . ."

Apple Muffins

1/4 cup shortening	1/2 teaspoon nutmeg
1/2 cup sugar	1/2 teaspoon cinnamon
1 egg	1 cup chopped apple
2 1/2 cups self-rising flour	1 cup milk

Cream shortening and sugar until fluffy. Add egg and beat well. Add dry ingredients which have been sifted together. Add apple, then milk, and stir. Fill well-greased muffin pans half full. Bake at 375° for 20-25 minutes.

Strictly For Boys

Shoo-Fly Coffeecake

4 cups flour	1/2 cup molasses
1 cup margarine	1/2 cup Karo
1 pound brown sugar	2 teaspoons soda
2 cups boiling water	

Combine flour, margarine and sugar; make crumbs. Set aside 1 1/2 cups crumbs for topping. Mix the remaining ingredients and add flour mixture. Pour into a greased and floured pan. Add crumbs on top. Bake for 45 minutes at 350°.

500 Favorite Recipes

Coffee Cake

1/2 cup margarine or butter
1 cup sugar
2 eggs
2 cups flour
1 teaspoon baking soda

1 teaspoon baking powder
1 cup sour cream
1 teaspoon vanilla
Light brown sugar, nuts, and
   cinnamon

Cream butter and sugar; add eggs. Sift flour with baking soda and baking powder. Add to creamed mixture alternately with sour cream. Add vanilla. Pour into a greased and floured 13-inch pan and top with light brown sugar, nuts, and cinnamon in quantity desired. Bake at 350° for 25-30 minutes. Cut in squares and serve hot with butter.

Nell Graydon's Cook Book

Pineapple-Walnut Bread

1 large can crushed
   pineapple
2 cups flour
1/2 cup sugar
3 teaspoons baking powder
1 teaspoon salt

1/2 teaspoon baking soda
3/4 cup chopped walnuts
1 egg
1/4 cup butter (melted)
1 1/2 teaspoons vanilla

Preheat oven to 350°. Grease a 9x5x3-inch loaf pan. Drain pineapple well. Into large bowl sift flour with sugar, baking powder, salt, and soda. Add walnuts, mix well. Add egg, pineapple, butter and vanilla with wooden spoon, stir just until blended. Turn into pan. Bake 1 hour or until cake tester comes out clean. Cool in pan on wire rack. Slice thinly. Then slice into 1/2-inch strips. Place on serving plate.

Carolina Cuisine

Harness racing is only one of three different horse races during Aiken's Triple Crown—a series of equestrian events spread over three weekends in March. Also a popular social event is the Carolina Cup held in Camden.

Zucchini Bread

2 eggs
1 cup sugar
1/2 cup oil
1 cup grated unpeeled
  zucchini
1 teaspoon vanilla

1 1/2 teaspoons cinnamon
1/2 teaspoon soda
1/2 teaspoon salt
1/8 teaspoon baking powder
1 1/2 cups flour

Beat eggs, sugar, and oil together. Add zucchini and vanilla.
Mix rest of ingredients together and add to zucchini mixture
until blended. Bake in a greased and sugared loaf pan at 350°
1 hour. Sprinkle the top with a little sugar.

Flavored With Tradition

Strawberry Bread

3 cups all-purpose flour
1 teaspoon baking soda
1/2 teaspoon salt
1/2 tablespoon ground
  cinnamon

2 cups sugar
3 eggs, beaten
1 cup vegetable oil
2 (10-ounce) packages frozen
  strawberries (thawed)

Combine first five ingredients and mix well. Combine eggs,
oil, and strawberries. Mix well and add to dry ingredients.
Pour batter into 2 greased and floured 9x5x3-inch loaf pans.
Bake at 350° for 1 hour or until a wooden pick inserted in the
center comes out clean. Yields 2 loaves.

Feeding the Faithful

Lemon Tea Bread with Blueberries

1/4 cup plus 2 tablespoons
  butter or margarine,
  softened
1 cup sugar
2 eggs
1 1/2 cups plain flour
1 teaspoon baking powder

Pinch of salt
1/2 cup milk
1 heaping tablespoon grated
  lemon rind
1 cup blueberries (fresh or
  frozen)

Cream butter. Add sugar until well blended, then add eggs. Begin adding flour, baking powder and salt. Add some milk then rest of flour. Stir in lemon rind and blueberries. Bake in greased loaf pan for 55 minutes at 350°.

GLAZE:

1/3 cup sugar
3 tablespoons lemon juice

2 teaspoons grated lemon
  rind

Combine sugar, lemon juice and lemon rind in saucepan and heat until sugar dissolves. (Works well in microwave also). Punch holes in top of baked loaf and pour mixture over warm bread. Makes one loaf, but it is so good you might as well go ahead and make two and freeze one.

One Course At A Time

French Bread with Cheese

1 long loaf French bread
1 (8-ounce) package sliced
  Swiss cheese, cut into
  thirds
1/2 cup margarine,
  softened

1 tablespoon prerpared
  mustard
1/4 cup onion, minced
2 tablespoons poppy seeds
2 slices bacon, cooked and
  crumbled

Preheat oven to 375°. Cut bread into individual servings by slicing almost all the way through the loaf vertically. Place cheese between bread slices. Combine margarine, mustard, onion and poppy seeds. Spread top and sides of bread with mixture. Place loaf in a foil "boat" and top with bacon. Bake 15 minutes. Serves 8-12.

Stir Crazy!

Virginia's Skillet Cheese Bread

2 tablespoons poppy seeds
2 tablespoons dried onion
  flakes
2 cups sharp cheese, grated

3 cups Bisquick
1/2 cup melted shortening
1 cup milk
2 eggs, beaten well

Mix first four ingredients. Add shortening, then milk, then eggs. Mix well. Line greased skillet or other pan with waxed paper. Grease again. Bake at 350° for 25 minutes or 'til golden brown. Butter surface. Serve immediately. May be frozen for later use.

Catch-of-the-Day

Macy's Bread Sticks

Hot dog buns
Melted butter

Rosemary or thyme

Split hot dog buns lengthwise so that each bun is 4 sticks. Dip into melted butter and sprinkle with either rosemary spice or thyme spice. Lay onto cookie sheet and bake at 300° for 30-45 minutes or until toasted. Let cool. Excellent with soups, salads or as an appetizer with beverages.

Cooking on the Go

Jalapeño Corn Bread

3 cups corn bread mix	1 large onion, diced
2 tablespoons sugar	1 (8 1/4-ounce) can
3 eggs, beaten	cream-style corn
2 cups milk	1 (4-ounce) jar diced
1/2 cup vegetable oil	pimento, drained
6 slices bacon, cooked and	2 tablespoons minced
crumbled	jalapeño peppers
1 1/2 cups (6 ounces)	
shredded sharp Cheddar	
cheese	

Combine corn bread mix and sugar in large bowl. Add eggs, milk, and oil, mixing well. Stir in remaining ingredients. Pour batter into a greased 13x9x2-inch baking pan. Bake at 400° for 40-45 minutes or until done. Serves 12.

Island Events Cookbook

Spinach Corn Bread Puff

10 1/2 ounces frozen chopped	1 medium onion, chopped
spinach	1 (8-ounce) carton cottage
1 (7-ounce) box corn bread	cheese
mix	1/2 teaspoon salt
4 eggs, beaten	
6 tablespoons butter, melted	

Thaw spinach and squeeze out all the water. Combine spinach and all remaining ingredients. Stir just until moistened. Pour into greased 9-inch pie plate. Bake at 400° for 25 minutes or until lightly browned. Serves 6.

Uptown Down South

Squashpuppies

Squash	Cornmeal/flour mixture
1 - 2 eggs, depending on amount of squash	Salt and pepper or other seasonings
Onion, chopped	

Cook as many squash as you desire. Add the eggs, chop onion into the mixture, then add enough cornmeal/flour mixture to thicken the squash. Season to taste. Cook in deep hot oil as you would hushpuppies. These will not be as round as hushpuppies, but make a delicious dish to eat with fish or anything.

Southeastern Wildlife Cookbook

Cheese Soufflé

1/4 cup flour	3 eggs
1/4 cup butter	Salt and pepper to taste
1 cup sweet milk	A light teaspoon mustard
1 cup grated cheese	(optional)

Prepare white sauce with flour, butter and milk. Add cheese and cook until thick. Add well beaten yolks of three eggs, salt, pepper and mustard. Mix carefully and fold in stiffly beaten whites of eggs.

Pour into a greased baking dish and set in a pan of hot water. Bake at medium heat 400° until firm. Will take about 30-40 minutes. Will serve 6 nicely.

Culinary Crinkles

 Six golf courses opened along the Grand Strand in 1987, bringing the total number of courses open to the public up to 46. In terms of both quantity and quality, the Grand Strand truly is the "Seaside Golf Capital of the World."

Breakfast Casserole

2 tablespoons melted butter	1/4 cup chopped onions
2 tablespoons flour	1/2 pound bulk sausage,
2 cups milk	crumbled
1/2 teaspoon salt	3 tablespoons melted butter
1/8 teaspoon pepper	1 dozen eggs, beaten
1 cup shredded medium	1 (4-ounce) can mushrooms,
Cheddar cheese	drained

Combine the 2 tablespoons of butter and flour. Blend until smooth. Cook over low heat until bubbly. Gradually stir in milk. Cook until smooth and thickened, stirring constantly. Add salt, pepper and cheese; heat until cheese melts, stirring constantly. Set aside. Sauté onions and sausage in the 3 tablespoons of butter until onion is soft and sausage is cooked. Add eggs. Cook until set stirring occasionally to scramble. Fold in mushrooms and cheese sauce. Spoon mixture into lightly greased 12x7x2-inch baking dish—may top with a can of crumbled French fried onions. Bake for 30 minutes at 350°. Serves 8. This recipe may be prepared ahead and refrigerated until time to bake.

Variation: Use 1 cup (4 ounces) diced Canadian bacon instead of sausage. Prepare as above. Mix 4 teaspoons melted butter, 2 1/2 cups soft bread crumbs (3 slices), 1/8 teaspoon paprika. Sprinkle on top. Cover, chill until 30 minutes before baking. Bake uncovered 30 minutes at 350°.

Carolina Cuisine Encore!

Alice's Brunch Casserole

1 pound sausage
1 (8-ounce) can crescent
  rolls
1 pound Monterey Jack
  cheese, shredded

5 eggs
3/4 cup milk
2 teaspoons minced onion
Garlic salt to taste

Fry and drain the sausage. Place roll dough flat in the bottom of a 9x13-inch pan to make a crust. Sprinkle sausage, then cheese over dough. Mix eggs, milk, onion and garlic salt in bowl. Pour mixture over the cheese layer. Bake at 350° for 20-25 minutes. Yield: 6-8 servings.

  Note: This casserole may be made the day before it is to be cooked.

Prescriptions for Good Eating

Molly Morgan's Tuna Casserole Sandwich

1 (6 1/2-ounce) can tuna
  fish
3 tablespoons mayonnaise
3 tablespoons sliced
  mushrooms
5 coarsely chopped black
  olives

2 hoagie rolls
Commercial thousand island
  dressing
6 tablespoons grated Cheddar
  cheese
4 asparagus spears

Drain tuna well and put it in a small bowl. Add mayonnaise, mushrooms and black olives, mixing until well combined. Split hoagie rolls in half, and spread each with thousand island dressing. Distribute tuna mixture evenly over each roll . Divide cheese over each half and top with asparagus. Place hoagie rolls on a baking sheet and bake 4-5 minutes in a 500° oven until the hoagies brown. Serves 4.

South Carolina's Historic Restaurants

McIntosh Sandwich

8 slices of bread, buttered   **8 slices of ham**
4 slices of fresh apples,   **Cinnamon and sugar**
** with peeling**   **8 slices of Swiss cheese**
Butter

Butter slices of bread. Cover with slices of unpeeled, thinly sliced apples. Dot with butter. Cover with ham. Sprinkle with cinnamon and sugar mixture. Put in hot oven for 3-4 minutes, until butter melts and sandwich is hot. Place Swiss cheese on top and put under broiler until cheese melts. Serve open-faced while hot. Add corn chips for a delicious meal. Serves 4.

Cooking on the Go

Medieval Scottish games of strength and agility, bagpipe performances, dancers and fair booths are among the activities of the September Scottish Games and Highland Gathering held in Charleston.

Reuben Loaf

3 1/4 cups all-purpose flour	6 ounces thinly sliced
1 tablespoon sugar	corned beef
1 teaspoon salt	1/4 pound sliced Swiss
1 package rapid rising yeast	cheese
1 cup hot water (125° - 130°)	1 (8-ounce) can sauerkraut,
1 tablespoon butter	well drained
1/4 cup thousand island	1 egg white, beaten
dressing	Caraway or cumin seeds

Set aside 1 cup flour. In a large bowl, mix remaining flour, sugar, salt, and yeast. Stir in hot water and butter. Mix in only enough of the reserved flour to make a soft dough; knead 4 minutes. On a greased baking sheet roll out dough to 10x14-inch rectangle. Spread dressing down the center third of the horizontal rectangle. Top with corned beef, cheese and sauerkraut. Cut the remaining dough into 1-inch strips from the filling to the end on each side of the filling. Alternating sides, fold strips at an angle over the filling. Cover dough with a light towel and place baking sheet over a large shallow pan half filled with boiling water for 15 minutes. Remove towel and brush top and sides of dough with egg white and sprinkle with seeds. Bake in preheated oven at 400° for 25 minutes. Let loaf cool for 5 minutes before cutting. Cut into 4 equal pieces. Serves 4 generously.

Please Don't Feed the Alligators

 Symbol of Sumter, the Opera House was originally built in 1872. In the heart of the city, it features a 100-foot tall tower with a precisely accurate clock operated by weights.

Vegetables

The Town Hall/Opera House on Main Street in Sumter.

Asparagus Soufflé

1/4 pound of butter
3 heaping tablespoons of
  flour
3 cups of milk
Salt
Pepper
2 (No. 303) cans of
  asparagus spears

2 cups grated sharp Cracker
  Barrel cheese
1/2 cup whole pecans or
  almonds
Paprika

Melt butter, stir in flour until well blended, add milk a little at a time and cook until creamy and thick. Season with salt and pepper. Put a layer of asparagus in greased casserole, then a layer of cheese and cover with cream sauce. Continue with layers until casserole is filled. Top with cheese and nuts and sprinkle with paprika. Bake at 350° for about 30 minutes until cheese is light brown. Serves 8-10.

Carolina Cuisine

Baked Beans

1 pound dry beans
1/2 pound bacon
1 medium onion, chopped
1 1/2 tablespoons salt

1 cup brown sugar
1/2 cup white sugar
1/2 cup catsup
1 pint tomato juice

Soak beans overnight, cook until tender. Drain and add remaining ingredients. Bake 2-3 hours at 350°.

500 Favorite Recipes

 The Lowcountry starts with the sandhills and goes down a broad, even plain to the tidewater. Its ancestry is mostly English, French Huguenot and African. The Upcountry is composed of a narrow strip of the Blue Ridge mountains and a Piedmont section. Its decendents are predominately English, with a sprinkling of Scotch, Irish, Dutch, and German.

Hot Marinated Green Beans

Delightfully different.

2 (16-ounce) cans green beans	1 cup sugar
3/4 cup vinegar	4 strips bacon
	1 medium onion, sliced

Cook beans in saucepan approximately 20 minutes. Drain and set aside. Bring vinegar and sugar to a boil. Remove from heat. Fry bacon and set aside. Add bacon drippings to the sugar mixture. Put beans in 1-quart baking dish. Slice onions over beans. Pour sugar mixture over top. Bake at 350° about 30 minutes or until onions are cooked. Crumble the bacon and put on top of casserole. Yield: 6 servings.

Prescriptions for Good Eating

Swiss String Beans

3 (10-ounce) packages frozen French-style string beans	2 teaspoons sugar
3 tablespoons butter or margarine	1 teaspoon salt
	1 pint sour cream
4 tablespoons onion, chopped	6 ounces Swiss cheese, grated
2 tablespoons all-purpose flour	1 small package slivered almonds (optional)

Cook string beans according to package directions. Drain. Make a cream sauce by melting butter over low heat and adding onion, flour, sugar, salt and sour cream. In a 2 1/2-quart casserole, layer beans, sauce, cheese and almonds. Repeat layers. Bake at 350° for 25 minutes. Serves 8-10.

Stir Crazy!

Broccoli Casserole

1 can cream of mushroom
  soup
1 cup mayonnaise
1 cup grated sharp Cheddar
  cheese
2 eggs, beaten

2 packages frozen chopped
  broccoli, cooked and
  drained
Enough Ritz cracker crumbs
  to cover top of casserole

Mix first four ingredients together and then fold in the broccoli. Top with Ritz cracker crumbs and bake at 350° for 30 minutes. Use 13x9x2-inch pan.

Feeding the Faithful

Broccoli with Hollandaise Sauce

STEAMED BROCCOLI:
1 bunch broccoli, stems
  peeled and tied

1 teaspoon salt

Place in pot in upright position. Bring water level to the base of flowerets. Add sugar and bring water to boil. Cook about 10 minutes, or until stem near head is tender. Remove and drizzle with melted butter or margarine. One bunch normally serves 4.

HOLLANDAISE SAUCE:
2 egg yolks
1/4 cup butter or margarine,
  melted
1/4 cup boiling water

1 tablespoon lemon juice
1/4 teaspoon salt
Dash cayenne

Water in bottom pan of double broiler should be no more than 1-inch deep. You do not want boiling water to touch the upper pot. Bring water to boil on high heat; reduce to medium heat. In top pan of double boiler, beat egg yolks lightly with wire whip. Stir in melted butter. Add boiling water slowly, stirring constantly until sauce thickens. Remove immediately, stir in lemon juice, salt and cayenne.

Southern Vegetable Cooking

Broccoli Parmesan

1 bunch fresh broccoli	1/2 teaspoon dry mustard
3 tablespoons butter	3 tablespoons plain flour
2 tablespoons minced onion	1 chicken bouillon cube
3/4 teaspoon salt	2 1/2 cups milk
Dash pepper	1/2 cup grated Parmesan
1/8 teaspoon marjoram	cheese

Cook broccoli in salted water until just tender. Arrange broccoli in shallow baking dish. Sauté onion in butter in a saucepan. Add seasonings and flour. Mix well. Add bouillon cube and milk. Cook, stirring constantly until mixture thickens and comes to a boil. Add cheese and stir until melted. Pour sauce over broccoli; sprinkle with paprika, and add 2 additional tablespoons Parmesan cheese. Bake in 375° oven 20 minutes or until browned.

Carolina Cuisine Encore!

Braised Red Cabbage

I prepared mounds of this cabbage while at the Hofbrauhaus on Hilton Head Island, S.C.. For a meal with a German accent, team it with Rindsrouladen and Potato Pancakes.

1 red cabbage (about 2 pounds) or 2 large cans	2 teaspoons salt
	2 teaspoons pepper
1/4 cup chopped onion	1/4 cup vinegar
1/4 cup lard or duck fat	1/4 cup brown sugar
1/2 cup applesauce	Lemon juice
1/4 teaspoon caraway seeds	

Remove the hard core and shred the cabbage. Soak it in cold water for 15 minutes, then drain.

In a large, covered pot, sweat the cabbage and onion in lard over low heat for about 20 minutes, until limp. Then add the applesauce, caraway seeds, salt, pepper, vinegar, and brown sugar.

Simmer, covered, for 1 hour and 20 minutes, or until tender. (When using canned red cabbage, cook for about half the time specified.) If the liquid has not been absorbed when the cabbage is done, uncover and cook slowly until it disappears. Finally, taste for salt, and add a touch of lemon juice. Yield: 8 servings.

A Journal of Fine Cooking

 Octoberfest celebrates the town of Walhalla's German heritage.

Carrot Casserole
Zesty!

2 1/2 pounds whole carrots, peeled
1/2 cup mayonnaise
1 tablespoon minced onion
1 teaspoon prepared horseradish
Salt and pepper to taste

1/2 cup finely crushed saltine crackers
2 tablespoons butter or margarine
1 tablespoon chopped parsley
Paprika

Preheat oven to 375°. Cook carrots in boiling water until fork tender. Drain. Reserve 1/4 cup liquid. Cool. Cut carrots lengthwise in narrow strips. Arrange in 9-inch square baking dish. Combine reserved cooking liquid with mayonnaise, onion, horseradish, salt and pepper. Pour sauce over carrots. Sprinkle cracker crumbs on top. Dot with butter or margarine. Sprinkle with parsley and paprika. Bake for 20 minutes. Serves 8.

Calories 187.78, Protein 1.88gm, Fat 14.67gm, Carbohydrates 13.69gm, Fiber 1.45gm, Cholestertol 18.48mg, Saturated Fats 3.69gm, Iron 1.01mg, Calcium 53.20mg, Sodium, 327.31mg, Potassium 331.80mg, Vitamin A 14403.00 I.U., Vitamin C 9.34mg, Thiamine 0.07mg, Riboflavin 0.08mg, Niacin 0.76mg

The Enlightened Gourmet

Greylogs' Very Very Carrots

1 pound young carrots
3 stalks celery with leaves
1 small onion, minced
1/3 cup sugar

2 tablespoons butter
3/4 cup sweet vermouth
1 cup seedless green grapes, halved

Peel carrots and slice into 1/4-inch pieces. Finely dice the celery stalks and leaves. Place all ingredients except grapes in a medium saucepan with the vermouth. Cover and cook over low heat until just barely tender, about 15-20 minutes. (Add a tablespoon of water if necessary.) Before serving, add the grape halves and heat for one minute, stirring until heated. Serves 4.

South Carolina's Historic Restaurants

Eden's Flower

1 head cauliflower,
  separated into flowerets
1 cup water
1 1/2 teaspoons salt
1 stick butter
1/4 teaspoon coarse ground
  black pepper
1 generous teaspoon basil

1 generous teaspoon oregano
2 cloves garlic, pressed
Juice of 1/4 lemon
3 medium zucchini, sliced
  1/2-inch thick
1/2 cup grated Parmesan
  cheese

In skillet, poach cauliflower in water with 1/2 teaspoon salt, about 5 minutes. Pour off water, remove flowerets. Melt butter in skillet, stir in seasonings (do not forget other 1 teaspoon salt). Add zucchini first, then cauliflower. Cover. Cook on low heat for 20 minutes, stirring occasionally. Toss with 1/2 cup Parmesan cheese before serving.

A Taste of South Carolina

Vegetable Casserole

1 (16-ounce) can French cut,
  drained green beans
1 can shoepeg corn
1/2 cup onion, chopped

1/2 cup sour cream
1 can cream of chicken soup
1/2 cup cheese, shredded
Salt and pepper to taste

TOPPING:
1 package (or 1 stack) Ritz
  crackers, rolled fine
1 stick margarine

1/2 cup slivered almonds
  (optional)

Mix together first 6 ingredients. Place crackers, margarine and almonds in fry-pan and stir until oleo is melted, do not brown. Spread on top of vegetables and bake at 350° for 45 minutes.

500 Favorite Recipes

Corn Casserole

2 tablespoons chopped onion
2 tablespoons flour
1/2 teaspoon salt
2 tablespoons oleo or
  butter

1 cup sour cream
2 (12-ounce) cans whole
  kernel corn
6 slices bacon, fried and
  crumbled

Sauté onion, flour and salt together with 2 tablespoons oleo or butter. Mix sour cream and corn. Blend and bring to a boil. Add to onion mixture and pour in greased baking dish. Sprinkle with crumbled bacon. Bake at 350° for 30-45 minutes. Serves 6-8.

Cooking...Done the Baptist Way

 The town of McCormick was named in honor of the inventor of the reaper, Cyrus H. McCormick, who donated the land where a large portion of the town was built.

Collard Greens

Do not season collards until they have cooked down, as it is very easy to have a heavy hand with the salt and pepper.

3 pounds collard greens,
  washed and chopped
2 cups water

1/2 pound side meat or ham
  bone or 1 ham hock
1 tablespoon white vinegar

Put ingredients into pot, cover, bring to a boil, reduce heat to simmer and cook 45 minutes or until tender. Serve to 4 with homemade corn bread.

CORN BREAD:
1 egg
1 1/2 cups whole milk
3 tablespoons vegetable oil
  or bacon drippings

2 cups plain yellow cornmeal
3 teaspoons baking powder
1 teaspoon salt

Combine egg, milk and vegetable oil in bowl. Add remaining ingredients and stir until smooth. Dot muffin pan with vegetable oil or bacon drippings. Preheat pan in oven about 3 minutes, remove and pour in batter—about 2/3 full. Place in oven preheated to 425° and bake 20-25 minutes.

Southern Vegetable Cooking

Barley-Mushroom Casserole

1/4 cup butter or margarine	2 beef bouillon cubes
1/2 cup finely chopped onion	1 quart boiling water
1/2 pound fresh mushrooms	1 cup regular barley
or canned sliced mush-	1 teaspoon salt
rooms, drained	

In a skillet over low heat, melt the butter. Add the onion and mushrooms and cook, stirring often until wilted. Dissolve the bouillon cubes in the boiling water. Into an ungreased 2-quart ovenproof glass or similar casserole (about 8 x 2 3/4-inch) turn the barley and salt. Stir in the onion and mushroom mixture and the bouillon. Bake uncovered in a 350° oven, stirring several times, for 1 hour. Cover, bake for 30 minutes more at 350°. Makes 8 servings. Good served with pork chops and steaks.

The Museum Cookbook

My Favorite Fried Okra

2 cups okra, 1/2-inch slices	2 cups milk
Salt and pepper	2 cups cracker meal
1 egg	2 cups vegetable oil

Salt and pepper to taste. Mix egg and milk. Dip okra into mixture and dust lightly with cracker meal. Place mealed okra on platter or cookie sheet. Heat oil (375°) to bubbling (important!) in skillet or electric fry pan before adding okra. Oil should cover okra. Fry until golden brown. Drain in colander or on paper towels. Place in bowl as you do popcorn, and salt lightly. Serve as a snack or vegetable dish to 4.

Southern Vegetable Cooking

Eggplant and Zucchini Oriental

An interesting combination of two vegetables.

2 tablespoons oil
3 small shallots or onions,
  cut up
3 medium tomatoes,
  skinned, cut up
6 large mushrooms, cut up
1 clove garlic, chopped
1 bay leaf

1 bell pepper, chopped
1/2 pound zucchini (4 large
  or 6 small), cut into bite
  size pieces
1 large eggplant, cut into
  bite size pieces
12 ounces Monterey Jack
  cheese, shredded

In heavy fry-pan, put 2 tablespoons oil, onions, tomatoes, mushrooms, garlic, bay leaf and bell pepper. Cook covered for 10 minutes. Add zucchini and eggplant. Cook for 15 minutes covered tightly. Pour into large baking dish. Cover with cheese and bake at 350° for 5-10 minutes. Serves 6.

Charleston Receipts Repeats

Mushroom Casserole

1 pound fresh mushrooms,
  quartered
1 large onion, diced
4 tablespoons butter
2 tablespoons flour
1 cup sour cream

1 teaspoon salt
1/4 teaspoon nutmeg
1/2 teaspoon pepper
2 tablespoons fresh parsley,
  minced

Sauté mushrooms and onions in butter until onions are soft. Sprinkle flour over mixture and cook 3-5 minutes, stirring constantly. Add sour cream, stirring constantly for 2 minutes. Add salt, pepper, nutmeg, and parsley. Transfer to a greased 2-quart casserole. Bake at 350° for 30 minutes until bubbly. Serves 6.

Please Don't Feed the Alligators

Eggplant Parmigiana

1 large eggplant, unpeeled
Salt and pepper
1 cup dry bread crumbs
2 eggs
Cooking oil to fry (olive
  oil preferred)
1 1/2 cups tomato sauce,
  heated to spread evenly

1/2 pound cheese of your
  choice, (sliced
  Mozzarella is the classic
  cheese for this dish)
1 teaspoon crumbled dried
  basil
1/2 cup Parmesan cheese,
  grated

Wipe eggplant clean and cut in 1/4-inch circular slices. Season with salt and pepper. Dip into bread crumbs, then in lightly beaten eggs, and again into bread crumbs. Place individually on cookie sheet and refrigerate 30 minutes. Heat lightly oiled skillet and fry slices until brown and tender. Drain on absorbent paper towels. Next, lightly butter baking dish; pour in some of the tomato sauce, spreading evenly. Arrange eggplant slices over the sauce. Cover with a layer of cheese, more sauce and a sprinkling of basil. Repeat procedure until dish is filled. Top with Parmesan. Bake in preheated 350° oven 25-30 minutes.

Southern Vegetable Cooking

Dilled New Potatoes

16 small new potatoes,
  washed but not peeled
1/2 cup butter, melted

3 tablespoons fresh dill weed
Salt to taste
Pepper to taste

In a large saucepan cover potatoes with cold water. Place on
high heat and boil 20 minutes or until fork tender. Drain.
Place in a serving bowl, toss in butter, dill, salt, and pepper.
Elegant, simple, and delicious! Serves 8.

Please Don't Feed the Alligators

Shrimp Stuffed Baked Potatoes

6 medium baking potatoes
1 stick butter or margarine
1/2 cup half-and-half
6 tablespoons finely chopped
  green onion

1 1/2 cups shredded Cheddar
  cheese
1 teaspoon salt
1 1/2 pounds shrimp, peeled
  and cooked

Wash potatoes; bake at 425° for 60 minutes or until done. When
cool to touch, cut potatoes in half lengthwise. Carefully scoop
out pulp, leaving a shell of about 1/4-inch thickness.

In a large bowl mix potato pulp, butter, half-and-half, onion, cheese and salt. Whip until smooth. By hand, stir in
shrimp. Stuff well with potato mixture. Bake at 425° for 15
minutes. Garnish with 1 or 2 whole shrimp.

One Course At A Time

On December 20, 1860 in Charleston, the Ordinance of Secession
was passed, making South Carolina the first state to secede from
the Union. The federally garrisoned Fort Sumter in Charleston
Harbor fell soon after to the Confederates and remained in their hands
until the evacuation of Charleston in 1865.

Grandma's Sweet Potato Pone

2 cups sweet potatoes
1/4 cup butter or margarine
1 teaspoon grated lemon rind
1/4 teaspoon ground ginger
1/4 teaspoon cinnamon
1/4 teaspoon cloves

1/2 teaspoon salt
1 cup brown sugar, firmly
  packed
2 eggs, well beaten
1/2 cup coarsely chopped
  nuts

Grate potatoes with fine grater; combine with next 7 ingredients. Add to well beaten eggs; blend. Pour into greased 1-quart casserole; top with nuts. Bake at 350° for 1 hour. Serve warm. Yields 4 servings.

The Museum Cookbook

Potato Pie in Orange Shells

6 or 8 orange skins
1 pound boiled scraped
  yellow sweet potatoes,
  well mashed
1/4 pound butter

5 eggs
1/2 pint milk
Grated peel and juice of 1
  lemon
Sugar to taste

Hollow oranges. Combine ingredients and put potato filling in shells and bake at 350° for 20 minutes or until juice begins to come from oranges.

Charleston Recollections and Receipts

Spinach Soufflé

3 tablespoons butter or
 margarine
1/4 cup all-purpose flour
1 teaspoon salt
1/4 teaspoon black pepper
1/8 teaspoon nutmeg

1 cup light cream
1/4 pound grated Swiss
 cheese
1 cup drained, finely
 chopped cooked spinach
3 eggs, separated

Melt butter and blend in flour, salt, pepper, and nutmeg. Add cream gradually, stirring until well blended. Cook over low heat, stirring, until mixture is thick and smooth. Add cheese and spinach, and cook until cheese is melted. Remove from stove and cool. Beat egg whites with electric beater until stiff. Separately, beat egg yolks until thick and lemon-colored. Add yolks to spinach mixture. Fold in beaten whites. Pour into a lightly buttered 1 1/2-quart soufflé or casserole dish. Bake in preheated 325° oven 45-50 minutes. Serves 4-6.

Southern Vegetable Cooking

Baked Vidalias Au Gratin

8 medium-size Vidalia
  onions, peeled and sliced
  1/4-inch thick, about 6 cups
2 tablespoons butter, or as
  needed
1/2 cup heavy cream

1/4 cup dry cocktail sherry
1/8 teaspoon pepper
1/2 cup grated Swiss cheese
1/4 cup grated Parmesan or
  Romano cheese

Preheat oven to 375°. Sauté half of onions in 2 tablespoons butter in large frying pan over low heat, stirring occasionally. Cook only until limp, 5-10 minutes; do not brown or discolor. Remove to 1 1/2-quart baking dish with slotted spoon; sauté remaining onions, using more butter, if necessary. Add to onions in baking dish, along with cream, sherry and pepper. Stir to mix. Top with Swiss cheese and then Parmesan or Romano. Bake until top is a bit brown and all is bubbling hot, 15-20 minutes. Serves 6-8.

Island Events Cookbook

Hopping John

Hopping John, made of cow peas and rice, is eaten in the stateliest of Charleston houses and in the humblest cabins and always on New Year's Day. "Hoppin' John eaten then will bring good luck" is an old tradition.

1 cup raw cow peas (dried
  field peas)
4 cups water
2 teaspoons salt

1 cup raw rice
4 slices bacon fried with 1
  medium onion, chopped

Boil peas in salted water until tender. Add peas and 1 cup of the pea liquid to rice, bacon with grease and onion. Put in rice steamer or double-boiler and cook for 1 hour or until rice is thoroughly done. Serves 8.

Charleston Receipts

Creamy Squash Casserole

1 1/2 pounds yellow squash, sliced
3/4 cup grated sharp Cheddar cheese
1 cup sour cream
4 ounces pimentos, drained and sliced
8 1/2 ounces raw, scraped Jerusalem artichokes (or water chestnuts), sliced

1 medium onion, finely chopped
1 stick butter
4 ounces of buttered, salted bread crumbs

Cook the squash in salt water until tender and drain well. Mix squash, cheese, sour cream, pimentos, water chestnuts, and onions, stirring gently.

Place in 2-quart baking dish and dot with butter. Sprinkle bread crumbs on top. Bake at 350° for 30 minutes. Serves 8.

Charleston Recollections and Receipts

Crowd Pleasing Casserole

2 - 3 cups squash
1 onion, chopped
2 carrots, grated
1 egg, slightly beaten
1/2 stick butter, sliced
1/2 cup mayonnaise
1 tablespoon sugar

1 cup grated Cheddar cheese, divided
1 - 1 1/2 cups cracker crumbs, divided
Dash cayenne pepper
Salt and pepper
Oregano

Put well-drained, hot squash in large mixing bowl. Add onion, carrots, egg, butter, mayonnaise, sugar, half of cheese, and half of cracker crumbs. Season with cayenne pepper, salt, pepper, and oregano. Mix all ingredients well. Put into buttered 1 1/2-quart casserole and top with remaining cheese and crumbs. Bake at 350° for 20 minutes.

Island Events Cookbook

Squash Casserole

4-5 medium squash (any
  summer squash)
Salt and pepper
2 egg whites
1/2 cup sour cream
3 strips cooked bacon,
  crumbled

1/4 cup pimiento,
  chopped
1 cup toasted bread crumbs,
  mixed with 1 tablespoon
  melted margarine
1 (2-ounce) can sliced
  mushrooms

Scrub whole squash in cold water, being careful not to break the skin. Place in unsalted boiling water and cook until fork can easily be inserted—about 5 minutes. Remove, drain and slice 1/4-inch thick. Salt and pepper each side lightly. Layer bottom of baking dish with squash. Separate egg whites from yolks. Beat whites slightly with fork, fold in sour cream and frost squash. Sprinkle some bacon and pimiento over first layer. Repeat layers until squash are used. Sprinkle top with bread crumbs, and garnish with mushrooms. Pace covered dish into preheated 400° oven and cook 30 minutes. Serves 4-6.

Southern Vegetable Cooking

Zucchini Stuffed with Almonds and Cheese

3 (8x2-inch) zucchini
1 1/2 tablespoons cooking
 oil
1/4 cup finely minced onion
1/2 - 2/3 cups dry fine
 crumbs from any sweet
 bread

2 ounces grated Swiss cheese
1 large egg, beaten
1/2 cup heavy cream
2 1/2 ounces ground almonds
3 pinches powdered cloves
3 tablespoons butter melted

Wash, trim ends and halve zucchini lengthwise. Parboil until tender-crisp; drain. When cool, scoop out center pulp and arrange shells in buttered casserole. Chop pulp. Put oil in skillet and sauté onion, covered, until clear.

Uncover, raise heat and stir in zucchini flesh and cook for several minutes. Add 1/3 cup bread crumbs, all but 3 tablespoons of the cheese and the egg. Mix thoroughly. Season to taste and add cream, almonds and cloves. Fill each half with stuffing and shape into a dome. Mix together remaining bread crumbs and cheese and sprinkle over each shell. Dribble butter over top. Bake in upper third of a 400° oven for 25-30 minutes until bubbling hot and browned on top. Serve from baking dish. Serves 6.

A Taste of South Carolina

Crock Pot Macaroni

1 (8-ounce) box macaroni,
 cooked
1 block sharp Cheddar
 cheese, grated
1 can evaporated milk

1 1/2 cups milk
1 stick oleo
3 eggs, beaten
Salt and pepper

Grease crock pot. Mix all ingredients. Cook on low for 4 hours.

Cooking...Done the Baptist Way

Linguine With Artichokes

6 tablespoons olive oil
5 tablespoons stick butter
1 teaspoon flour
1 cup chicken stock or broth
1 clove garlic, crushed
2 teaspoons lemon juice
1 teaspoon minced parsley
Salt and pepper to taste

8 artichoke hearts, cooked
  and drained
3 tablespoons fresh grated
  Parmesan cheese
1 teaspoon drained capers
1 pound linguine
2 tablespoons olive oil
1/4 teaspoon salt

In a large heavy skillet, heat 4 tablespoons olive oil over moderately low heat. Add 4 tablespoons butter, and after melted, add 1 teaspoon flour. Cook, stirring for 3 minutes. Stir in heated chicken stock. Increase heat to moderately high. Cook sauce for 1 minute. Add garlic, lemon juice, parsley, and salt and pepper. Cook over moderately low heat for 5 minutes, stirring occasionally. Add artichoke hearts, 2 tablespoons Parmesan cheese, capers. Cover sauce, basting hearts several times, and cook 8 minutes. Cook linguine in 6 quarts salted water al dente. Drain in colander. In another pot, combine 2 tablespoons olive oil, 1 tablespoon Parmesan cheese, 1 tablespoon butter, 1/2 teaspoon salt. Return linguine to pot and toss with artichoke mixture. Top with sauce. Serves 4.

Charleston Receipts Repeats

Macaroni Pie

3/4 cup uncooked macaroni
1/4 stick margarine
3 eggs

1 pound cheese
1 1/2 cups milk

Boil macaroni in salted water until tender. Drain and add margarine. Add eggs and cheese. Reserve enough cheese to garnish top. Add milk and season to taste.

The Sandlapper Cookbook

Stuffed Shells Florentine

1 cup ricotta cheese
1 cup shredded mozzarella
　cheese
1/4 cup grated Parmesan
　cheese
1 egg, slightly beaten
1 (10-ounce) package frozen
　chopped spinach, cooked
　and well drained

1/2 teaspoon dried crushed
　oregano leaves
1/4 teaspoon salt
1/2 box jumbo shell macaroni
　(about 20), cooked al dente,
　drained, and cooled
1 (15 1/2-ounce) jar Prego
　spaghetti sauce
Chopped parsley

In a bowl, mix first seven ingredients. Stuff about 2-3
tablespoons cheese mixture into each shell. In a 12x8-inch
baking dish, spread half of the Prego. Arrange shells, stuffed
side up, in sauce. Spoon remaining sauce over shells. Cover
with foil. Bake at 350° for 35 minutes or until hot. Sprinkle
with chopped parsley. Yield: 4 servings. This is a good family
dish. I serve it with garlic bread and a frozen fruit salad for a
wholesome favorite meal.

Per Serving: Calories 552; Protein 30 g; Cholesterol 149 mg; Sodium 1140mg;
　Fiber 2.08 g
Percent of Calories: Protein 21%; Carbohydrates 32%; Fat 47%

Palmetto Evenings

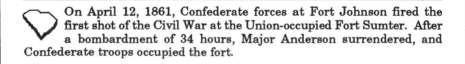

On April 12, 1861, Confederate forces at Fort Johnson fired the
first shot of the Civil War at the Union-occupied Fort Sumter. After
a bombardment of 34 hours, Major Anderson surrendered, and
Confederate troops occupied the fort.

Spinach Fettuccine with Broccoli and Almonds

1 (12-ounce) box spinach
  fettuccine, or fresh if you
  have access to it
10 - 12 strips bacon
1 large onion, diced
1 cup fresh mushrooms,
  sliced

1 head fresh broccoli cut
  into bite-size pieces
1 cup half-and-half, scalded
1/4 cup Parmesan cheese
1 small pack sliced almonds

Cook fettuccine according to directions. Drain. Fry bacon in skillet, remove to drain on paper towel. Sauté onion and mushrooms for 2 minutes. Steam or boil broccoli, leaving crisp-tender. Run under cold water to prevent further cooking. Pour half-and-half (hot) over noodles, tossing lightly. Add mushrooms, crumbled bacon, onions, and broccoli. Toss all lightly. Sprinkle with Parmesan cheese and almonds. Serve on heated plates. Will serve 6 as main course.

One Course At A Time

Bluffton Spinach Delight

1 (3-ounce) package cream
  cheese (room temperature)
1/2 cup mayonnaise
1 tablespoon lemon juice
1/2 teaspoon dry mustard
2 pounds cooked shrimp

2 cans cream of mushroom
  soup
2 packages frozen, seasoned,
  cooked and drained
  spinach
Parmesan cheese

Mix first six ingredients together. Pour mixture into drained spinach. Sprinkle with Parmesan cheese and bake at 350° for 1 hour. This recipe serves eight.

Bluffton's Favorite Recipes

Pecan Pilaf

1/2 cup butter or margarine
1 cup pecans, chopped
1/2 cup onion, chopped
2 cups long-grain rice,
  uncooked
2 cups canned chicken broth
2 cups water
1/2 teaspoon salt

1/4 teaspoon dried thyme,
  crumbled
1/8 teaspoon rosemary
1/8 teaspoon freshly ground
  pepper
3 tablespoons fresh parsley,
  chopped
1 cup carrots, grated

Melt 3 tablespoons butter in a large skillet over medium-high heat. Add pecans, and sauté 2-3 minutes or until lightly browned. With a slotted spoon, transfer pecans to a small bowl. Cover and set aside.

Melt remaining butter in the same skillet. Add onion, and sauté 5 minutes or until tender. Add rice, and stir 2 minutes or until evenly coated.

Meanwhile, bring broth, water, salt, thyme, rosemary, pepper and 2 tablespoons parsley to a boil in a saucepan over medium-high heat. Add mixture to rice. Cover, reduce heat to low and simmer 20 minutes or until liquid is absorbed. Add pecans, carrots and remaining parsley. Fluff with a fork and serve. Serves 12-14.

Stir Crazy!

Broccoli Rice Quiche

1 1/2 cups cooked rice
1 egg, beaten
3/4 cup (3 ounces) shredded
   cheese, divided
1 (10-ounce) package frozen
   chopped broccoli

2 teaspoons minced onion
1/3 cup milk
2 eggs, beaten
1/4 teaspoon pepper
1 (4-ounce) jar sliced
   mushrooms, drained

Combine rice, 1 egg and 1/2 cup cheese, mixing well. Press mixture into a greased 9-inch pie plate; set aside. Cook broccoli according to package directions; drain well. Add 1/4 cup cheese and remaining ingredients to broccoli; mix well. Pour broccoli mixture into rice lined pie place. Bake at 375° for about 50 minutes, or until done. Yields one 9-inch quiche.

Olivia's Favorite Menus and Recipes

Vidalia Onion Quiche

3 tablespoons margarine
1/4 cup Vidalia onions,
   sliced
1/2 cup diced ham*
1 pie crust, unbaked,
   pricked
1 1/2 cups Cheddar cheese,
   grated

1 cup Swiss cheese, grated
1 cup caraway seed cheese,
   grated
1/4 cup evaporated milk
3 eggs
1/2 cup sour cream
1/2 cup crumbled bacon

Melt margarine in a skillet and sauté onions and ham until done. Place in bottom of unbaked pie crust. Mix cheeses, milk, eggs, and sour cream and pour atop onion and ham mixture. Bake at 350° for 30 minutes and garnish with crumbled bacon. From the Gracious Gourmet.

*1 can minced clams may be substituted.

Island Events Cookbook

 Though onions are sold worldwide as vegetables, they really belong to the lily family.

Herbed Rice

2 1/2 cups chicken broth
1 cup uncooked, long grain
 rice
3 tablespoons margarine or
 butter

2 tablespoons dried chives,
 chopped
1/4 teaspoon basil
1/4 teaspoon savory
1/4 teaspoon garlic salt

Bring chicken broth to boil; stir in rice, cover, reduce to simmer and cook until done—30 minutes. While rice is cooking, melt margarine in saucepan, add herbs and garlic salt, stir and heat. Remove cooked rice to serving bowl and mix in seasoned margarine. Serves 4-6 persons with either fried, baked, broiled or poached fish.

Southern Fish and Seafood Cookbook

Fried Rice

2 tablespoons oil
2 eggs, slightly beaten
2 strips bacon, diced
2 scallions, finely chopped
1/4 teaspoon sugar

1 teaspoon salt
2 tablespoons soy sauce
3 cups cold cooked rice
1 cup chopped ham

Heat skillet or wok on high heat for 30 seconds. Pour in 1 tablespoon of oil and swirl around pan. Pour in eggs and keep folding until they are lightly cooked. Transfer eggs to a bowl and break up. Pour the other tablespoon of oil into pan and sauté bacon and scallions until golden. Add egg and remaining ingredients and stir fry for approximately 3 minutes until all grains of rice are coated. Serve at once. Serves 4-6.

Flavored With Tradition

Brown Rice

2 tablespoons margarine　　　**1 can onion soup**
2/3 cup rice　　　　　　　　**1/2 soup can of water**
1 (4-ounce) can mushroom
**　pieces, drained**

Melt margarine in heavy saucepan. Add rice and mushroom pieces. Brown rice and mushrooms in melted margarine, stirring often. Add soup and water; bring to boiling. Reduce heat, cover, and simmer, stirring occasionally until rice is tender, about 25 minutes. Serves 6.

Strictly For Boys

Red Rice

1/2 pound bacon　　　　　　**Salt and pepper to taste**
1 pound rice　　　　　　　　**4 cups chicken broth**
1 small can tomatoes

Have the bacon sliced and cut in small pieces. Fry it until crisp and remove the bits of bacon. Leave about four tablespoons of the drippings and in this brown the rice, stirring constantly to see that it does not burn. Then add the tomatoes, a teaspoon of salt and the chicken stock. Cover closely and cook for half an hour or until the rice is tender. Add the bacon bits and serve, seasoning to taste with salt and pepper.

Two Hundred Years of Charleston Cooking

According to legend, rice was introduced to America around 1694 when a ship bound for England was forced to stop in Charleston for repairs. The ship's captain bartered for the costly repairs with a small portion of his cargo of rice. This inexpensive portion of a rather unexciting cargo was the beginning of the rice fields which were to line the swampy riverbanks from Charleston to Savannah.

Vegetable Pot Pie

2 carrots, cooked and diced
2 medium new potatoes, cooked and diced
1/2 cup field peas or butter beans, cooked

1/2 cup cooked corn, cut from cob
1/4 teaspoon black pepper
1 teaspoon salt
Pastry crust

SAUCE:
1/2 cup melted butter or margarine (fresh fat skimmed from boiling a baking hen is preferred, but not absolutely necessary)

1/4 cup all-purpose flour
2 cups chicken broth
1/2 cup whole milk

Melt butter in saucepan. Add flour and stir until paste becomes almond-colored. Stir in chicken broth. After sauce thickens, add milk. More milk may be needed. (This should be a medium sauce). Add vegetables and seasonings, folding in gently. Place in casserole. Cover with pastry crust, brush with melted butter or margarine and bake in preheated 425° oven until crust has lightly browned.

Southern Vegetable Cooking

Zucchini Pie

3 cups sliced zucchini
1 large chopped onion
1/2 cup sharp Cheddar cheese
1/2 cup Parmesan cheese
1/2 cup salad oil

1 cup Bisquick
4 eggs, beaten
1/2 teaspoon salt
1/2 teaspoon pepper

Combine all ingredients. Mix well. Pour into greased 9x9-inch baking dish. Bake 30-35 minutes at 350°. Can be divided into 2 baking dishes. This freezes well before baking.

Bethel Food Bazaar II

Tomato Pie

1 (9-inch) pie shell, baked and cooled	Sweet basil
	Chives
2 or 3 large tomatoes, thickly sliced	2 or 3 green onions, chopped
	1 cup mayonnaise
Salt	1 cup sharp cheese, grated
Pepper	

Fill pie shell with tomatoes. Sprinkle with salt, pepper, basil, chives and green onions. Mix mayonnaise and cheese. Spread over tomatoes. Bake for 30 minutes at 350°. Serves 6.

Sea Island Seasons

Spinach Pie

2 packages frozen spinach	1 egg, beaten
1 small onion	Muenster cheese, sliced
1/2 stick butter	1/4-inch thick
Garlic powder	
1 cup shredded Cheddar cheese	

Preheat oven to 350°. Defrost and squeeze water from spinach. Sauté onion in butter with garlic powder. Mix spinach in with onions, butter, and garlic. Pack half of mixture in ungreased pie pan and top with Cheddar. Then add the other half of the spinach mixture. Dribble egg, and top with Muenster slices. Bake at 350° for 30 minutes or until brown. Yield: 6-8 servings.

Per Serving: Calories 441; Protein 22 g; Fat 38 g; Cholesterol 149 mg; Fiber 1.9 g
Percent of Calories: Protein 19%; Carbohydrates 5%; Fat 75%

Palmetto Evenings

South Of The Border is a well-known tourist stop-off on I-95 just south of the state line. Visitors are directed toward its facilities by Pedro's famous billboards.

Broiled Peaches

Good with cured ham or pork.

FOR EACH SERVING:

1 peach	**Dash cinnamon**
1 teaspoon brown sugar	**1/2 teaspoon margarine**

Peel fresh peaches, halve and remove pit. Place in shallow baking dish. To each half add 1 teaspoon brown sugar, sprinkle with cinnamon and top with 1/2 teaspoon of margarine. Broil until mixture bubbles and peaches are lightly browned. Serve warm.

The Peach Sampler

Pickled Pineapple

Great with poultry or ham!

2 (20-ounce) cans sliced pineapple	**1 1/2 teaspoons whole cloves with heads**
1 cup pineapple juice	**2 (3-inch) cinnamon sticks, broken**
1 cup white vinegar	**Red cherries**
1 1/2 cups sugar	
Dash of salt	

Drain pineapple. In a large saucepan, bring to a boil 1 cup pineapple juice, vinegar, sugar, salt, cloves and cinnamon. Simmer 15 minutes. Carefully add the pineapple. Bring to a boil and simmer 5 minutes longer. Remove the cinnamon. Carefully overlap pineapple slices in two different directions in a 2-quart casserole. Decorate with cloves and cherries. Pour hot syrup over all. Cover and refrigerate at least 24 hours before serving. Will keep several weeks if refrigerated. Yield: 8-10 servings.

Note: Pineapple may be cut into chunks and used as an hors d'oeuvre.

Prescriptions for Good Eating

Pineapple Pudding

4 cups white bread crumbs	3 eggs
1/2 cup milk	1 large can crushed
1 stick margarine	pineapple, drained (canned
2 cups sugar	in its own natural juice)

Trim bread. Cut into cubes and soak in the 1/2 cup milk. Cream together margarine, sugar and eggs. Add crushed pineapple and bread crumbs. Mix well. Pour into greased casserole and bake at 350° until firm, about 30-40 minutes. Serve with whipped cream or whipped topping or plain. Cut into squares.

    Note: If desired, a little grated cheese may be added to mixture, or sprinkle a little on top the last 10 minutes of baking.

Olivia's Favorite Menus and Recipes

Hot Fruit Compote

12 dried macaroons, crumbled	1/2 cup toasted slivered almonds
4 cups fruit—peaches, pears, apricots, cherries, well drained	1/2 cup brown sugar
	1/2 cup cooking sherry
	1/4 cup melted butter

Butter a 2 1/2-quart casserole. Cover bottom with macaroon crumbs. Add layers of fruit. Top with macaroons. Sprinkle with almonds, sugar and sherry. Bake at 350° for 30 minutes. Add melted butter over top. Serve hot.

Cooking...Done the Baptist Way

Cranberry Relish

1 pound cranberries	1 3/4 cups sugar (or to
1/2 lemon	taste)
1 whole orange	1 cup chopped pecans

Put cranberries, lemon and orange (seeds removed) through food grinder. Add sugar and nuts; mix well. Chill before serving.

This is the perfect Thanksgiving and Christmas relish, but by freezing cranberries when they are in season, you can make this delicious recipe all year long.

Seasoned with Light

Cold Catsup
A relish.

1 1/2 pecks ripe tomatoes	1 tablespoon black pepper
6 large onions	1 cup mustard seed
8 large green peppers	1/4 cup salt (or less, if
1/3 bottle horseradish,	you prefer)
mixed with water to make	3 pints vinegar
a paste	

To peel tomatoes, drop for a minute or so in boiling water. After peeling, grind (or use food processor) in coarse mill with peppers and onions. Drain many times until juice is gone. (If you can't find powdered horseradish, use a little of the creamed horseradish, to taste.) Season the mix after draining. Do not cook. Seal in hot, sterile jars, airtight.

The vinegar keeps this from spoiling. Delicious with meats, hamburgers, hot dogs, greens, etc.

Seasoned with Light

South Carolina Cucumber Pickles

7 pounds cucumbers   **2 cups lime**

Slice cucumbers and cover with a solution made of 2 cups lime in 2 gallons of water. Let soak 24 hours, then rinse well. Cover with clear water and let soak 3 hours. Drain well, cover with the following mixture:

2 quarts vinegar   **1 teaspoon whole cloves**
4 1/2 pounds sugar   **1 teaspoon celery seed**
1 tablespoon salt   **1 teaspoon pickling spice**

Heat vinegar mixture until sugar melts. Put cucumbers in it and soak overnight, covered. Cook cucumbers in syrup for 35 minutes at boiling stage. Pour in hot jars while syrup is hot. Boil jars to seal for 5 minutes.

A Taste of South Carolina

The Pee Dee area of the state lies almost entirely within South Carolina's coastal plain. It is drained by the Great and Little Pee Dee, Black and Lynches rivers. Stephen Foster's original lyrics for his famous song read: *Way down upon the Pee Dee River....*

Spiced Tomato Jam

1/4 pound ripe tomatoes
1/4 cup lemon juice
1 1/2 teaspoons lemon rind, grated
1/2 teaspoon allspice, ground

1/2 teaspoon cinnamon, ground
1/4 teaspoon cloves, ground
4 1/2 cups (2-pounds) sugar
1 box powdered fruit pectin

Scald, peel and chop tomatoes. Cover and simmer 10 minutes, stirring occasionally. Measure 3 cups into 6 or 8-quart sauce pot. Add lemon juice, lemon rind and spices to tomatoes. Measure sugar and set aside. Stir pectin into prepared fruit. Bring to a full rolling boil over high heat, stirring constantly. Stir in sugar all at once. Stir and bring to a full rolling boil that cannot be stirred down. Boil hard 1 minute, stirring constantly. Remove from heat; skim with large metal spoon. Ladle immediately into hot, sterilized jars; seal. Process in canner 5 minutes if desired. Makes five 8-ounce jars.

The Sandlapper's Salvation Cookbook

Sea oats are dominant along the coast and serve as an integral part of the ecology of shore birds and prevent destruction of dunes by wind and sea. They are protected by law, and cutting or uprooting of the plant is prohibited.

Seafood

Sea oats wave in the ocean breezes along the 55-mile stretch of family beaches known as the Grand Strand.

Captain's Choice Flounder

1 1/2 sticks of margarine or
  butter
Bread crumbs
12 slices tomatoes
6 medium thick fillets
  of flounder, cut to fit
  tomato slices

Salt and pepper
Dill weed
Parmesan cheese
Lemon juice

Melt 3/4-stick of butter in bottom of 10x15-inch cookie pan. Sprinkle bread crumbs over butter in bottom of pan, place sliced tomatoes on crumbs, cover each with a piece of flounder, skin side down. Sprinkle with salt and pepper to taste and a fraction of dill weed, a generous coating of Parmesan cheese and then squeeze lemon juice over each and dribble the rest of the melted butter. Bake at 350° for 10 minutes and slip under the broiler to brown.

One Course At A Time

Baked Stuffed Flounder

3 or 4 large flounders
Lemon juice

1 stick butter

STUFFING:
2 tablespoons bacon
  drippings
2 cloves garlic, minced
3 tablespoons celery,
  chopped
1/4 cup bell pepper, chopped
1 cup crab meat

1 egg, beaten
1 teaspoon salt
1/8 teaspoon thyme
1 tablespoon parsley,
  chopped
1/2 teaspoon pepper
1 cup bread crumbs

Make a slit in one side of flounder. Sauté vegetables in bacon drippings, then mix with remaining ingredients. Stuff each fish. Melt butter with lemon juice in pan. Place fish in pan and cover with foil. Baste every 10 minutes. Bake at 375° for 30 minutes. Uncover last 5-10 minutes.

Recipes from Pawleys Island

Flounder with Crabmeat

Have 1 1/2 to 2 pounds flounder prepared and cut for stuffing. Baste flounder with Dill Sauce.

1 cup crabmeat
2 tablespoons bell pepper
1/2 stick butter
1 1/2 teaspoons
   Worcestershire sauce
1/2 teaspoon Sauer's
   seasoning salt

1/4 teaspoon black pepper
1 teaspoon lemon juice
1 tablespoon chopped parsley
Dash of Tabasco
1 cup bread crumbs mixed
   with 1/2 stick of melted
   butter

Sauté bell pepper in butter and add to crabmeat with other ingredients, Worcestershire sauce, seasoning salt, black pepper, lemon juice, chopped parsley and Tabasco. Stuff flounder and cover top of crabmeat where exposed with buttered bread crumbs. Bake at 350° for 5 minutes. Then turn on broiler for approximately 4-6 minutes to brown.

DILL SAUCE:
Salt and pepper
1/4 pound butter, melted

Juice of one lemon
2 teaspoons dill weed

Season fish with salt and pepper. Mix butter, lemon and dill weed and baste generously over fish while cooking.

"Don't Forget the Parsley...."

Flounder Vinaigrette

4 fillets from 1 1/2 - 2-
   pound flounder

1/4 cup melted margarine
   butter

Salt and pepper fillets to taste; baste with butter, place on broiler pan 4 inches from coils and broil 5-8 minutes per side.

VINAIGRETTE DRESSING:
1/2 cup olive oil
1 tablespoon white vinegar
1/2 teaspoon celery seed
1/2 teaspoon salt

1 teaspoon lemon juice
1 clove garlic
Dash thyme

Place ingredients in small saucepan; heat, remove garlic and pour over broiled fillets. Serves 4.

Southern Fish and Seafood Cookbook

Schooner Steaks Flamingo

2 pounds red snapper, or
  other fish steaks
1 teaspoon salt
Dash pepper
1 cup grated cheese
1 tablespoon prepared
  mustard

2 teaspoons horseradish
2 tablespoons chili sauce
1/4 cup butter or other fat,
  melted

Cut steaks into serving size portions. Sprinkle both sides with
salt and pepper. Combine cheese, mustard, horseradish, and
chili sauce. Place fish on a greased broiler pan about 2 inches
from source of heat. Brush with butter and broil 5-8 minutes
longer or until fish flakes easily when tested with a fork. Place
cheese mixture on top of fish. Return to broiler for 1-2 minutes or until cheese melts and browns. Serves 6.

Culinary Crinkles

Fish and Chip Bake

1 package instant potatoes
  (enough for 4 servings)
1 (10-ounce) package frozen
  chopped spinach, cooked
  and well drained
1/2 cup dairy sour cream
Dash of pepper
1 (16-ounce) package frozen
  perch fillets, thawed

1/4 cup milk
1/2 cup herb seasoned
  stuffing mix, crushed
2 tablespoons butter or
  margarine, melted
Lemon slices

Prepare potatoes according to package directions except reduce water by 1/4 cup. Stir in well drained spinach, sour cream
and pepper. Turn into a 10x6x2-inch baking dish. Skin fish
fillets. Dip one side of each fillet in milk, then in crushed stuffing mix. Fold fillets in halves, coating side out. Place atop
potato mixture. Drizzle with melted butter. Bake uncovered
at 350° till fish fillets flake easily when tested with a fork, 30-
35 minutes. Serve with lemon slices. Makes 4-5 servings.

Olivia's Favorite Menus and Recipes

Turbin of Sole

4 - 6 sole or flounder fillets	1/2 cup cracker or bread crumbs (or more) (with bread crumbs add a little salt and pepper)
1 tablespoon minced green onion and tops	
1 tablespoon fresh chopped parsley	1/2 pound crabmeat with juice
1 tablespoon chopped celery	1 egg
Sliver of garlic, minced	Fresh lemon juice
6 tablespoons melted butter	

Freshen fish in ice cubes. Dry well and cut fillets into 1 1/2-inch strips. Grease muffin tin with butter or margarine and fit fish strips in circle in each muffin hole. Chop vegetables together. Melt butter. Sauté vegetables until limp; then add bread crumbs and crabmeat. Cool slightly and add beaten egg. Stuff lined muffin cups and pour remainder of melted butter over each. Squeeze fresh lemon juice over each before eating. Bake at 350° for 10 minutes, or until done.

Thoroughbred Fare

Zippy Fish Fillets

2 pounds fillets, fresh or frozen
1/4 cup melted butter or margarine
1 teaspoon salt

1 teaspoon grated onion
1 teaspoon paprika
2 tablespoons lime juice
Dash of pepper

Arrange fillets, cut in serving pieces, in greased baking dish. Mix remaining ingredients together. Pour over fish. Preheat oven to 450°. Bake in center of oven uncovered for 10-12 minutes per inch of thickness. Fold under the thinner ends for more even cooking. Bake 20-24 minutes per inch of thickness for frozen fish.

MicroBaking: Place in shallow nonmetallic container. Microwave uncovered for 3-5 minutes per pound on HIGH. Rotate frequently for even cooking and test for doneness after 2/3 time has lapsed. Place thickest parts toward the outside or fold under the thinner ends for more even cooking. Let stand 1-2 minutes. Season or sauce after cooking to avoid dehydration of fish. Microwave frozen fish 9-15 minutes per pound.

Catch-of-the-Day

Baked Fish Daufuskie

DAUFUSKIE CHEESE SAUCE:

2 ounces heavy cream	Dash Worcestershire sauce
2 ounces coarse grain country mustard	Dash Tabasco
1/2 cup Cheddar cheese	Salt
2 ounces cooked crumbled bacon	Pepper

FISH:

8 ounces fresh grouper	1/2 ounce bread crumbs
3 ounces sliced mushrooms, sautéed	3 ounces Daufuskie Cheese Sauce

Make sauce by heating cream in heavy skillet. Add ingredients of sauce. Whisk until smooth over medium heat. Bake grouper at 350° until almost cooked. Add sauce, sautéed mushrooms and bread crumbs. Return to oven till bread crumbs brown. Serve with lemon wedge. From Old Fort Pub, Hilton Head Plantation.

Island Events Cookbook

Broiled Crappie with Sweet-and-Sour Dressing

4 whole cleaned crappies	Salt and pepper to taste
1 cup bottled sweet-and-sour dressing	Orange slices

Marinate crappies in sweet-and-sour dressing for 1 hour. Remove, salt and pepper, and place on broiler pan 4 inches from coils. Broil 8-10 minutes per side. Serves 4. Garnish with fresh orange slices when served on platter.

Southern Fish and Seafood Cookbook

Baked Trout with Wine-Almond Sauce

4 (1/2 - 1-pound) whole
cleaned trout

1/4 cup melted margarine or
butter

Salt and pepper trout; brush with melted margarine, place in pan and bake 5 minutes per pound per side.

WINE-ALMOND SAUCE:

1 cup almonds
1 cup water
1/2 cup melted margarine
or butter

1/2 cup white wine

Blanch almonds quickly in boiling water. Remove, peel and either shave or chop fine. Melt margarine or butter in saucepan. Add almonds and brown. Blend with wine and pour over baked trout on serving platter. Serves 4.

Southern Fish and Seafood Cookbook

Salmon Loaf

1 cup salmon
1 cup cracker crumbs
1/4 teaspoon celery salt
1/4 teaspoon pepper
1/2 teaspoon salt

2 eggs
1 cup milk
2 tablespoons butter
(melted)

Mix all ingredients and pour into buttered loaf pan. Bake at 350° for 30 minutes. Serves 4.

The Sandlapper Cookbook

 Boaters from across the nation compete at the D.F. Jenkins Memorial Boat Races in Eutawville each June.

Baked Sea Bass with Spinach and Bread Stuffing

3 or 4 dressed sea bass,
  fresh or frozen
2 1/2 teaspoons salt
1 1/2 cups celery, thinly
  sliced
1/4 cup green onions, sliced
1/2 cup butter or margarine,
  melted

4 cups soft bread cubes
  (1/2-inch)
4 cups fresh spinach leaves,
  washed, well-drained
1 tablespoon lemon juice
1/4 teaspoon pepper

Thaw fish if frozen. Clean, wash and dry fish. Sprinkle inside and outside with 1 1/2 teaspoons salt. Cook celery and onions in six tablespoons butter or margarine until celery is tender. Stir in bread cubes and spinach leaves. Cook and stir until spinach is tender. Add lemon juice, remaining one teaspoon salt, and pepper; toss lightly. Stuff fish loosely. Close opening with small skewers. Place fish in well-greased baking pan. Brush with remaining butter or margarine. Bake in a moderate oven, 350° for 40-60 minutes or until fish flakes easily when tested with a fork. Makes 6-8 servings.

Southeastern Wildlife Cookbook

Pawleys Island Inn Crab Cakes

1 cup homemade mayonnaise
1/8 teaspoon cayenne pepper
1 egg white
Juice of 1/2 lemon

3 tablespoons extra fine
  cracker meal
1 pound fresh lump crabmeat
1 stick butter

Blend mayonnaise, pepper, egg white, lemon juice and cracker meal; then fold lightly into crabmeat. Shape into patties and roll in fresh bread crumbs. Sauté in heavy skillet with butter until evenly browned. Drain on absorbent towel before serving.

Recipes from Pawleys Island

Crab Cakes

In South Carolina, Daufuskie Crab Cakes tend to be made with plenty of breading and seasoning. This recipe, though, is lots of flaky crabmeat with just enough moistened bread crumbs added to simply hold the meat together.

3 slices white bread, day
  old works best
1 pound lump crabmeat
2 tablespoons mayonnaise

1 teaspoon dry mustard
1 teaspoon parsley
1 egg

Break bread into crumbs. Gently mix with all other ingredients until thoroughly combined. Shape into patties. Pan fry in butter until brown and cooked through. Serves 2-4.

Hudson's Cookbook

 Keep live crabs on ice in cooler, but not in water, as they need oxygen. Never cook a dead crab. Throw him out if he's not moving.

Deviled Crab

1 dozen large crabs (1 to 1
  1/2 pounds meat)
4 boiled eggs, chopped fine
2 stalks celery, chopped
  fine

Salt, pepper, mace
2 large tablespoons
  mayonnaise
Bread crumbs
Butter

Boil the crabs twenty minutes. Remove from heat, cook and pick. Be careful to remove "dead man" meat and fat. Use only the white meat and the claw meat.

Lightly add four boiled chopped eggs, chopped celery, a little salt, pepper and mace (to taste) with mayonnaise. Put mixture lightly in crab shells. Lightly cover with crumbs which have been salted. Put a lump of butter on the top of each shell. Put in a large biscuit pan or shallow baking pan. Bake in 350° oven for 15-20 minutes or until hot. *Do not* burn the tops or let the meat dry out. Put a dab of chutney on top. Serve immediately. Makes 8 deviled crabs.

Charleston Recollections and Receipts

Deviled Crab

1/2 stick margarine
1/2 small onion, chopped
1 stem celery, chopped
1/2 bell pepper, chopped
3 eggs, beaten
12 Ritz crackers, crumbled
  slightly
1 heaping tablespoon
  mayonnaise

1 teaspoon prepared mustard
1 tablespoon Worcestershire
  sauce
1 dash Tabasco sauce
1/2 teaspoon salt
Black pepper
1/4 cup milk
1 pound claw crabmeat

Melt margarine in heavy saucepan. Sauté onion, celery, and pepper until tender, but not browned. Beat eggs, add all other ingredients, and toss together lightly until well mixed. Turn into 1-quart casserole, sprinkle with additional cracker crumbs, and paprika. Bake at 325° about 25-30 minutes or until firm. Serves 6.

Strictly For Boys

Crabmeat Thermidor

For a luncheon, serve this in patty shells.

1/2 cup chopped onion
1/4 cup chopped green pepper
2 tablespoons butter
1 (10-ounce) can frozen
  cream of potato soup,
  thawed
3/4 cup light cream
1 1/2 cups shredded sharp
  Cheddar or Swiss cheese
2 teaspoons lemon juice

2 (6-ounce) packages frozen
  crabmeat, or 2 cans
  crabmeat, drained
3 tablespoons sherry
1 (8-ounce) can sliced water
  chestnuts, optional
Paprika
Minced parsley

Sauté onion and green pepper in butter until tender but not brown. Add soup, then cream. Heat slowly, stirring constantly, until heated but not boiling. Stir in cheese until melted. Remove from heat. Add lemon juice, crabmeat, sherry and water chestnuts. Reheat. Serve over toasted Holland Rusk, patty shells or individual ramekins. Garnish with paprika and parsley. Yield: 6 servings.

Note: Shrimp may be substituted for crabmeat; cream of shrimp soup may be substituted for potato soup.

Prescriptions for Good Eating

Meeting Street Crab Meat

4 tablespoons butter
4 tablespoons flour
1/2 pint cream
Salt and pepper to taste

4 tablespoons sherry
1 pound white crabmeat
3/4 cup sharp grated cheese

Make a cream sauce with the butter, flour and cream. Add salt, pepper and sherry. Remove from fire and add crabmeat. Pour the mixture into a buttered casserole or individual baking dishes. Sprinkle with grated cheese and cook in a hot oven until cheese melts. Do not overcook. Serves 4. (1 1/2 pounds of shrimp may be substituted for the crab).

Charleston Receipts

Stuffed Crabs and Mushrooms

2 tablespoons butter	Juice of 1/2 lemon
1 cup mushrooms	1 teaspoon capers
1 tablespoon flour	1 teaspoon chopped parsley
1/2 cup cream	2 egg whites, beaten stiff
1 pound cooked crabmeat	

Melt the butter and add the mushrooms, sliced or chopped. Cook until they are tender. Remove the mushrooms or put them to one side of the pan and add the flour. When that is well blended, add the cream. When the cream sauce is thick, remove from the fire and add the other ingredients in the order given. Put the mixture back into the crab shells, or if the shells are not available (this dish is delicious made from canned crabmeat!).

Bake in a buttered casserole in a moderate oven (350°) for about twenty minutes. Serves 8.

Two Hundred Years of Charleston Cooking

 Five of the world's eight species of swans glide along the black swamp waters at Swan Lake Iris Gardens in Sumter, where Dutch and rare Japanese iris surround the lake with vivid color.

Mrs. C.A. (Wallis) Houseman's Crab Quiche

Baked pie shell	2 beaten eggs
6 ounces crabmeat	1/2 cup cream
2 green onions, chopped	1/2 teaspoon salt
1/4 pound Swiss cheese	Dash dry mustard,
1/2 cup mayonnaise	pepper and
1 tablespoon flour	Lea & Perrin sauce

Prick and bake pie shell for 6 minutes at 400°. Mix all other ingredients. Pile into partially baked pie shell. Sprinkle with almonds. Bake at 350° for 35 minutes. Makes appetizer in small wedges or luncheon dish in larger portions.

Recipes from Pawleys Island

 South Carolina's inland lakes boast some of the best fishing in the southeast. Crappie, bluegill, panfish, catfish, and white, striped, hybrid and large-mouth bass are prominent throughout the state.

Scallops Provençale

6 tablespoons olive oil
2 cloves garlic, finely
  chopped
1 shallot, finely chopped
1 1/2 pounds scallops,
  rinsed, dried, quartered

1 teaspoon lemon juice
1 dash Tabasco, optional
1 large tomato, peeled and
  chopped
Salt and pepper
1/4 cup parsley

Heat oil in heavy skillet. Sauté garlic and shallot until tender but not brown. Increase heat and add scallops. Sauté scallops until lightly browned and opaque—about 5 minutes. Add lemon juice, Tabasco, tomato, salt, pepper and parsley. Cook long enough to heat thoroughly. Serves 4-6.

Sea Island Seasons

Coquilles Saint-Jacques

1 1/2 pounds scallops,
  cut in chunks
1 tablespoon shallots,
  chopped
1/4 teaspoon salt
Dash white pepper
1/2 cup dry vermouth or
  sauterne

1 cup heavy cream
1 tablespoon flour
4 tablespoons butter,
  softened
Parmesan cheese, freshly
  grated
Parsley, freshly chopped
  (optional)

In 2-quart saucepan bring scallops, shallots, salt, pepper and vermouth to a boil. Cover. Simmer 2 minutes. Remove scallops with slotted spoon. Reduce remaining liquid to half by cooking about 10 minutes. Add cream. Boil rapidly 'til syrupy. Lower heat. Combine flour and butter, then stir into liquid, cooking 'til thickened.

Remove saucepan from heat. Return scallops to cream sauce, stirring to coat evenly. Divide equally among shell ramekins (ideal molds for homemade pastry shells), purchased pastry shells or shallow casserole. Top with Parmesan and parsley. Heat at 450° for 5 minutes or until golden bubbly. Serves 4-8.

Variation: This recipe is exceptional with chunks of fish, crab or shrimp. May be frozen for later use.

Catch-of-the-Day

Lobster Cardinale

8 live lobsters, 1 1/4 - 1
  1/2 pounds each
1/4 cup unsalted butter
2 tablespoons chopped
  shallots

1/4 cup sliced mushrooms
1 tablespoons brandy
2 tablespoons seasoned bread
  crumbs
Optional - truffle peelings

Remove claws from the live lobster by grasping firmly and twisting. Boil claws in salted water for 8 minutes. Drain, cool, crack, and remove meat from claws and reserve. Also reserve all shells from the claws. Place lobster bodies on a sheet pan. Place a brick or similarly heavy object on top at the end of the tail portion to keep flat. Bake in 400° oven for 8 minutes. With kitchen shears cut in 2-inch wide section of the top shell the entire length of the lobsters. Remove tail meat, vein and rinse under running water. Reserve meat. Rinse out remainder of lobster body being careful not to break in two. Refrigerate while making sauce.

SAUCE:
1/4 cup chopped onions
1/4 cup chopped celery
1/4 cup brandy
3 tablespoons tomato juice
4 sprigs fresh parsley with
  stem

1 tablespoon fresh chopped
  thyme or 1/2 teaspoon dried
3 pints heavy whipping
  cream

Place claw shells, onion and celery in a saucepot. Cook 5 minutes, stirring so as not to burn vegetables. Add brandy and flame. Add tomato juice, parsley and thyme. Cook covered 5-8 minutes on low heat. Add cream. Bring to a boil and simmer 20 minutes. Strain sauce and keep warm.

  Melt butter in a large sauté pan. Add shallots and mushrooms; cook 2 minutes until soft. Add lobster meat (claws and tails); sauté 2 minutes.

CONTINUED

CONTINUED

Add brandy and flame, stirring cautiously. Add sauce to the sauté pan and cook until it thickens slightly (3-5 minutes maximum). With a slotted spoon carefully spoon lobster mixture into shell cavities, top off each with remaining sauce and sprinkle lightly with bread crumbs and truffle peeling (optional).

Bake at 500° for 2 minutes until browned. Transfer to a serving platter. From Mrs. Iris Campbell, First Lady of South Carolina.

Palmetto Evenings

Lobster Sauce

Probably nothing will earn you the reputation of a chef par excellence quicker than a dish of quenelles (or fish mousse) swimming in a sinfully rich Lobster Sauce. This is a Fish Velouté enhanced with Lobster Butter. It can be poured over almost any fish. Serve over fish mousse, with or without cooked shellfish as a garnish.

FISH VELOUTÉ:

1/2 cup white wine
1 cup clam juice or fish stock
1 1/2 tablespoons chopped shallots
2 bay leaves
2 tablespoons butter
3 tablespoons flour
1 cup heavy cream
1 tablespoon lemon juice
Salt and white pepper to taste

In a 2-quart sauce pot, bring to a boil the wine, clam juice or stock, shallots, and bay leaves.

In a separate saucepan, melt the butter with the flour, stir, and cook for 3 minutes on low heat, until it turns a straw color. Add to the boiling stock. With a wire whip, beat until smooth. Cook slowly, uncovered, for 5 minutes to further cook the flour and thicken. Add the heavy cream. Simmer gently over low heat, uncovered, for 5 minutes. Season with lemon juice, salt, and white pepper.

LOBSTER BUTTER:

1 live Maine lobster (1 1/4 pounds)
2 tablespoons butter
2 tablespoons salad oil
1/2 cup white wine
1 stick (1/4-pound) unsalted butter, softened
1 1/2 tablespoons tomato paste

Split the live lobster down the middle and sauté in the 2 tablespoons butter and the oil in a large covered skillet for 5 minutes. If live lobsters upset you, steam for 5 minutes, then split and sauté. Remove the lobster from the skillet and deglaze the skillet with white wine. Strain into the Fish Velouté. Let the lobster cool and remove all meat from the shell. It is not necessary that the meat come out in large chunks. Save the tomalley and the roe, and put them with the lobster shells (discard any large shells; save only the thin legs and white body shells). Crack the claws and extract the claw meat, discarding the hard shells. Set the meat aside.

Place all thin shells in a food processor bowl, breaking any large pieces with your hand so as not to jam the blade. Add tomato paste and process until most of the shells are finely ground and form a paste.

Add the stick of butter (room temperature) and purée until pasty. Scrape down the sides of the food processor bowl. Place the Lobster Butter on a 14-inch-long piece of plastic wrap. Roll it up into a cylinder, and squeeze and twist both ends. Refrigerate.

To combine the Lobster Butter with the Fish Velouté, heat the Velouté in a skillet or saucepan until bubbly. Cut 1/2 of the Lobster Butter into slices and whisk it into the Velouté over medium heat. (Freeze the remaining Lobster Butter for later use.) Do not let it boil. Remove from heat.

Strain into a double boiler and keep warm on low heat. (Straining is very important with this sauce because of the lobster shells not being completely dissolved. Be sure to strain before adding the lobster meat.) If the sauce begins to separate, add 2 tablespoons cream and stir with a wire whip. Dice the lobster meat and heat it in 2 tablespoons butter in a small skillet. Add it to the sauce. Yield: 2 cups.

A Journal of Fine Cooking

Since 1935, when a local fisherman began serving steamed oysters in a crude wooden shed, local families have been feeding hungry crowds in what has become known as Calabash style—usually meaning lots of lightly battered, deep fried seafood with heaps of hushpuppies on the side.

Stuffed Clams Normande

18 large clams
2 tablespoons finely chopped onion
3 tablespoons finely chopped mushrooms sautéed in butter for one minute or B & B canned mushrooms

1 teaspoon minced parsley
1 1/2 tablespoons minced chives
2 tablespoons fine bread crumbs
1 teaspoon sherry wine
White wine

Place the well scrubbed clams in a kettle with just enough water to cover the bottom. Cover the kettle and steam over hot flame until shells open. Remove the meat from the shells and discard the tough necks. Chop the clams finely and mix with the onion, mushrooms, chives, parsley and bread crumbs. Stir in the sherry and just enough dry white wine to moisten the mixture. Heap the mixture into the clam shells, sprinkle with buttered bread crumbs and bake at 350° for about 15 minutes or until crumbs are golden brown.

Recipes from Pawleys Island

Scalloped Oysters

1/2 cup stale bread crumbs
1 cup cracker crumbs
1/2 cup melted butter
1 pint oysters

Salt and pepper
4 tablespoons oyster liquor
4 tablespoons milk or cream

Mix bread and cracker crumbs; stir in butter. Put a thin layer of this mixture in bottom of shallow, buttered baking dish; cover with oysters and sprinkle with salt and pepper. Add half each, oyster liquor and milk or cream. Repeat and cover top with remaining crumbs. Bake 30 minutes at 450°. Use only two layers of oysters. You may sprinkle each layer with mace or nutmeg.

Recipes from Pawleys Island

Oyster Purlo

1/2 pound bacon	2 cups raw rice
1 medium onion, chopped fine	3 cups oyster (small ones better)
1/2 cup chopped bell pepper	2 cups oyster liquid
1/2 cup chopped celery	Salt and pepper to taste

Fry bacon until crispy. Crumble and set aside. Add onions to bacon fat, cook until transparent—remove and add to crumbled bacon. Fry celery and pepper, remove them and add to bacon and onions.

Heat oysters in pan until all water is expelled from them. Remove oysters and reserve 2 cups of liquid.

In pot wash rice, add the 2 cups of oyster liquid and all the other ingredients, including most of the bacon fat. (Go easy on the salt for the oysters are already salty.) Let come to a boil, stirring occasionally—without a lid.

After it boils, cover pot, lower fire to simmer and keep stirring occasionally. When all the liquid has been absorbed, place a paper towel between the top of the pot and the lid to hold any moisture that might collect. When rice is done, remove from heat. Enjoy.

Stirrin' The Pots On Daufuskie

Scalloped Oyster Pie

1 pint oysters (standard or selects)	Crumbled saltines
	Salt and pepper to taste
1 teaspoon lemon juice	1 Pint half-and-half cream
6 tablespoons melted butter	

Mix lemon juice and melted butter. Make layer of crumbled saltines, medium thickness. Add layer of half the oysters (liquor reserved). Sprinkle oysters with salt, pepper and butter. Repeat to form a second layer. Mix oyster liquid with half-and-half. Pour over casserole sufficient to moisten. Top with crumbled saltines. Refrigerate for 1 hour or longer. Bake at 350° for 30 minutes.

"Don't Forget the Parsley. . . ."

Shrimp Mariner's

2 pounds shrimp
  (16-20 count)
4 wooden or metal
  skewers
Salt and pepper

3/4 cup honey
1/4 cup Dijon mustard
1/2 stick melted butter
2 grapefruit (pink)
  sectioned

Place 8 shrimp on each skewer. Season with salt and pepper and drizzle with a little butter. Place under broiler until shrimp are firm (approximately 5 minutes) being careful not to burn tails. While they are cooking, combine honey, mustard and butter, hold on the side. Remove shrimp from skewer and arrange on plate alternating with grapefruit, starting and ending with shrimp. Pour sauce over shrimp, put under broiler just long enough to warm. Serve with rice. From Pisces at the Mariners Inn, Palmetto Dunes Resort.

Island Events Cookbook

Creole Shrimp

4 slices bacon
1/2 cup chopped onion
1/2 cup chopped celery
1/2 cup bell pepper
2 cups tomatoes
1/2 cup chili sauce

1 teaspoon Worcestershire
  sauce
1/4 teaspoon black pepper
4 shakes Tabasco sauce
1 teaspoon salt
1 pound boiled shrimp

Fry bacon and remove from pan. Put onion, celery and bell pepper in the bacon fat and brown lightly. Now, add tomatoes, chili sauce, Worcestershire sauce, black pepper, Tabasco and salt.

Cook slowly until thick, stirring occasionally. Add shrimp 30 minutes before serving. Break the fried bacon in small pieces and add last.

Go by taste. Add more seasoning if needed.

Recipes from Pawleys Island

Shrimp and Rice Casserole

1 1/2 cups chopped onion
3/4 cup chopped green
  pepper
1 1/2 sticks margarine
3 pounds shrimp, peeled
  and cooked
2 (4-ounce) cans mushrooms
  with juice

2 - 3 tablespoons
Worcestershire sauce
6 cups cooked rice
2 -3 cans mushroom soup
  (add 2 and more if
  necessary for consistency)
A few shakes of Tabasco

Sauté onion and pepper in margarine until soft. Add all ingredients and mix. Place in buttered baking dish and bake at 300° until thoroughly hot.

Seasoned with Light

Shrimping is the largest seafood industry in South Carolina. When buying shrimp, remember the head and shell total about half the shrimp's weight. Freeze shrimp in milk cartons in water to cover to prevent freezer burn.

Yellow Shrimp Risotto

2 tablespoons butter
1/2 cup thinly sliced celery
1 cup sliced fresh mushrooms
1/2 cup sliced green onions
  with tops
1 clove garlic, pressed
1/2 cup white wine
1 tablespoon soy sauce

1 teaspoon salt
1 teaspoon white pepper
1 pound fresh shrimp,
  shelled, cleaned, and
  cut in half
1 pint sour cream
1 cup yellow rice

Melt butter in large skillet or wok. Add celery, mushrooms, onions, and garlic, and sauté lightly. Add wine, soy sauce, salt, and pepper, and bring just to a boil. Add shrimp and stir until they all turn pink. Turn heat down and add sour cream. Cover and simmer 10 minutes. Serve over rice cooked according to package directions. Serves 4.

Please Don't Feed the Alligators

Lowcountry Fettucini

4 ounces fettucini
1 tablespoon pimentos, diced
1/4 pound small bay scallops
1/4 pound small shrimp, peeled
1/4 pound crabmeat
1/2 teaspoon salt
1/2 teaspoon pepper
1/3 stick butter
Sherry or white wine to taste (optional)
Garlic-Dill Cream Sauce
1/2 cup frozen baby green peas
Fresh parsley to garnish

Cook the fettucini according to the directions on the box about the same time as starting the sauce. Start the seafood about five minutes before the sauce and fettucini are done. The peas are best when lightly cooked. They may be placed in a wire mesh strainer or colander in the boiling fettucini water the last minute or two.

Sauté the pimentos, scallops, shrimp and crabmeat with the salt, pepper and butter in skillet until almost done (only 2-3 minutes). Stir in sherry or wine and cook until just done (about a minute more). Stir in the cream sauce and the peas and ladle over individual plates of fettucini. Serve immediately. Serves 2-3.

GARLIC-DILL CREAM SAUCE:
1/3 stick butter
1 tablespoon self-rising flour
1 cup half-and-half
1/2 teaspoon sugar
1/2 teaspoon dill weed, dried
1/2 teaspoon garlic powder

Melt butter in top section of double boiler. Add flour and stir well. Cook two minutes, stirring often. Slowly stir in the half-and-half and add the sugar, dill and garlic powder. Stir almost constantly as the sauce gradually thickens.

Southeastern Wildlife Cookbook

The East Bay Trading Company's Linguine with Shrimp

6 ounces linguine
2 tablespoons butter
1/2 tablespoon ground garlic
4 ounces tiny shrimp
1/2 ounce white wine

1 tablespoon fresh parsley
Salt and white pepper to taste
2 - 3 tablespoons Parmesan cheese

Cook linguine al dente. Rinse thoroughly with cold water and set aside. To a medium sauté pan, add butter, garlic and shrimp. Cook for one minute or until shrimp are done, adding the wine during the cooking process. Add linguine, parsley, salt, pepper and Parmesan cheese to shrimp, and toss thoroughly before serving. Serves 2.

South Carolina's Historic Restaurants

Charleston Shrimp Bake

1 cup onion, chopped
1 cup celery, sliced
1/3 cup margarine
1 can tomato wedges, undrained
3 cups cooked rice
1 teaspoon dill weed or oregano

1 pound peeled, deveined and cooked shrimp
4 ounces crumbled feta cheese
1/2 cup sliced black olives

Cook onion and celery in margarine until tender. Add tomato wedges and heat. Stir in rice, dill weed, shrimp, cheese and olives. Bake at 350° for 25 minutes or until shrimp are cooked. Makes 6 servings.

Southeastern Wildlife Cookbook

Shrimp and Scallop Sauté

6 green onions with tops, cut in 1-inch pieces

2 teaspoons minced garlic

1/2 cup butter or margarine, melted

1 pound fresh shrimp, peeled and deveined

3/4 pound fresh scallops

1/2 pound lump crabmeat

1/2 pound fresh mushrooms, sliced

1 (8-ounce) can sliced water chestnuts, drained

1/2 cup finely chopped green pepper

1 tablespoon plus 1/2 teaspoon salt-free herb and spice seasoning

1 tablespoon Worcestershire sauce

2 tablespoons chopped fresh parsley

Hot cooked rice (optional)

Sauté green onions and garlic in butter in a large, heavy skillet for 1 minute. Add remaining ingredients except parsley and rice. Cook over medium heat for 6-8 minutes, stirring occasionally. Stir in chopped parsley. Serve mixture over rice, if desired. Serves 6.

The Museum Cookbook

Shrimp Stuffed Bell Peppers

6 bell peppers, that will
  sit flat in a dish
1/2 pound bacon, cut fine
1 large onion, chopped
1 stalk of celery, chopped
1 1/2 pounds shrimp, cooked
  and peeled
1 egg
1 (5 1/2-ounce) can
  evaporated milk

1/2 cup milk
1/2 teaspoon salt and pepper
5 shakes Tabasco
1/2 teaspoon Worcestershire
  sauce
1/4 teaspoon mace
1/2 cup cracker meal plus
  enough for topping each
  pepper
3 - 4 teaspoons butter

Clean peppers by cutting off tops and removing membranes and seeds. Reserve tops. Boil peppers in boiling water for 2 minutes. Fry bacon; drain off all but 1 1/2 tablespoons of grease. Add the onions to the grease and sauté. Chop the tops of the bell peppers and add along with the celery to the mixture and sauté until light in color. Add shrimp and sauté 2-3 minutes. Cool. In separate container beat the egg, add milk, the shrimp mixture, seasonings, and cracker meal. Stuff the bell peppers with the shrimp and sprinkle with more cracker meal on top of each. Dot with butter. Bake at 375° for 45 minutes. This recipe can be doubled, made the day ahead or frozen. Do thaw before cooking. Serves 6.

Calories 441.51, Protein 40.45gm, Fat 21.86gm, Carbohydrates 19.76gm, Fiber 1.80gm, Cholesterol 262.63mg, Saturated Fats 8.13gm, Iron 5.02mg, Calcium 368.14mg, Sodium 685.01mg, Potassium 657.49mg, Vitamin A 1006.15 I.U., Vitamin C 111.92mg, Thiamine 0.22mg, Riboflavin 0.mg, Niacin 3.60 mg

The Enlightened Gourmet

 Oyster shells are used with salt marsh muck to make fertilizer, ground up with sand and water to make construction material (called "tabby"), and also ground up into chicken feed to make hen egg shells harder.

Shrimp Pie

1 teaspoon salt
2 cups day old biscuit
  crumbs or bread crumbs
1 large green pepper,
  chopped
2 cups shrimp, peeled and
  coarsely cut
1 teaspoon Tabasco

4 tablespoons catsup
4 tablespoons Worcestershire
  sauce
2 tablespoons prepared
  mustard
4 tablespoons butter, melted
2 cups milk

Add salt, bread crumbs, and green pepper to shrimp. Make sauce of remaining ingredients and pour over shrimp mixture. Let stand 1 hour. Bake covered at 350° for 40 minutes. Uncover and brown. Serves 6.

Sea Island Seasons

Capt'n 'Fuskie's Lowcountry Boil

6 pounds smoked sausage,
  cut in pieces
20 ears of corn, broken in
  half
1 pound butter
4 large onions, cut in
  chunks
4 bell peppers, cut in
  quarters

6 pods garlic
3 pounds Irish potatoes,
  scrubbed and left in their
  jackets Salt and pepper to
  taste
6 pounds shrimp, headed and
  washed

In huge pot, cook sausage in water for about 20 minutes. Add remaining ingredients except headed shrimp. Cook until potatoes are almost done. Add shrimp and cook until just tender.

Drain off water. Cover table(s) with newspaper. Take pot of "boil" and throw it out on the table(s) as though you were throwing out a bucket of water. Let everyone help himself, using paper plates. Have plenty of iced tea on hand and if you like, some slices of Vienna or French bread smeared with garlic butter. Plenty of paper towels will be needed as this "boil" is "drippin'-lickin'-good!"

Stirrin' The Pots On Daufuskie

Charleston Shrimp Breakfast

Venturing out on the ebb tide with cast net or seine and catching the small sweet creek shrimp is a favorite pastime. Properly prepared, they are an incomparable treat. A memorable breakfast menu features shrimp gravy over hominy alongside buttered toast with fig preserves, crisp bacon, slices of brilliant vine-ripened tomatoes, and a pot full of steaming coffee.

1 1/2 - 2 pounds fresh white or brown creek shrimp	**1/4 teaspoon ground black pepper**
3 - 4 tablespoons bacon fat	**2 - 3 tablespoons flour, maybe more**
2 tablespoons onions, finely chopped	**Hominy**

Pick and devein shrimp while still raw. If freshly caught, head them and refrigerate for about one hour to make shelling a bit easier. Bring three cups of water to a rapid boil and add the shrimp. Gently stir for about five minutes. Pour them into a colander, saving the liquid.

Heat fat in a large frying pan. Add onions and pepper. After about two or three minutes, add flour and stir around in the pan until all fat is absorbed and the mixture begins to turn brown. Pour on the liquid in which the shrimp was boiled and stir vigorously around the bottom of the pan.

After two or three minutes, stir in the shrimp, lower the heat, cover, and let simmer for 4-5 minutes before serving over hominy.

It is said that, upon first sampling this dish, one spontaneously lowers the head in a moment of silent prayer.

Southeastern Wildlife Cooking

The Spoleto Festival U.S.A. is an international arts festival which runs for 17 days and presents over 100 performers to nearly 100,000 people each spring in Charleston.

Curried Shrimp

1 pound fresh shelled shrimp	1 garlic clove, finely chopped
2 cups water	
1 teaspoon salt	1 teaspoon salt
1/2 teaspoon black pepper	1 1/2 tablespoons all-purpose flour
1 whole bay leaf	
1 tablespoon onion, finely chopped	1 1/2 tablespoons curry powder
1 1/2 tablespoons margarine or butter	1 cup canned whole tomatoes, chopped
1/2 cup onion, chopped	1 tablespoon lemon juice

Place shrimp in pot; add water, salt, pepper, bay leaf and onion. Bring to boil, cover, reduce to medium heat and cook 4 minutes. Strain and reserve 1 1/2 cups shrimp broth.

In skillet—medium heat—melt margarine or butter; add onions and cook until tender. While stirring, add garlic, salt, flour and curry powder. Cook 3 minutes, stirring. Add tomatoes, lemon juice and shrimp broth. Stir. Reduce heat to simmer and cook 10-12 minutes, covered. Add shrimp, heat and serve to 4 over steamed rice.

Southern Fish and Seafood Cookbook

Cha-Sha
Shrimp Fried in a Light Tempura Batter

2 ounces cornstarch
3 ounces sugar
1/2 teaspoon salt
1/2 teaspoon baking soda
Pinch of Accent
1 egg

1/3 cup oil
1/3 - 1/2 cup water
Drop of yellow food coloring
36 large shrimp, butterflied
8 ounces flour

Combine all dry ingredients except flour and mix well. Add egg and oil and enough water to get the consistency of pancake batter and add a drop of food coloring. Dredge large shrimp (butterflied) in flour, then in batter, and holding by the tail, drop shrimp gently into 450° deep fat fryer. Cook until golden color, turning occasionally. Serve with sweet and sour sauce. Serves 6.

If you don't use a deep fat fryer, it is almost impossible to handle the shrimp gently enough so that the batter doesn't crumble off.

Hudson's Cookbook

Shrimp Thermidor

1 pound cooked shrimp
1/2 cup sliced mushrooms
1/4 cup butter, or melted
   fat
1/4 cup flour
1 teaspoon salt

1/2 teaspoon dry mustard
Dash cayenne pepper
2 cups milk
Grated Parmesan cheese
Paprika

Cut large shrimp in half. Cook mushrooms in butter for 5 minutes. Blend in flour and seasoning. Add milk gradually and cook until thick, stirring constantly. Stir in shrimp. Place in well greased 6-ounce custard cups. Sprinkle with cheese and paprika. Bake in hot oven 400° for 10 minutes or until cheese browns. Serves 6.

The Sandlapper Cookbook

Seafood Triangles

6 ounces frozen crabmeat	1/8 teaspoon ground nutmeg
2 tablespoons butter	1/2 teaspoon salt
2 tablespoons onion, chopped	2 tablespoons dry sherry
2 scallions, chopped	8 tablespoons feta cheese
1/2 cup fresh mushrooms, chopped	1 tablespoons grated Parmesan cheese
1 cup Bechamel Sauce	1 egg yolk
2 tablespoons parsley, finely minced	1/2 cup cornflake crumbs
1/8 teaspoon dill weed	1/2 pound filo pastry
1/4 teaspoon red pepper	1/2 pound sweet butter, melted

Prepare Bechamel Sauce.

Thaw and drain crabmeat. (Reserve one tablespoon of liquid.) In large saucepan melt butter and sauté onion, scallions and mushrooms until tender, about three minutes. Remove from heat.

Slowly add Bechamel Sauce, stirring. Add all remaining ingredients (except filo and half-pound sweet butter). Return to very low heat and cook about five minutes until cheeses have melted. Stir in one tablespoon crab liquid. Set aside in refrigerator overnight or several hours (this will enhance the flavor and mixture will be easier to use).

BECHAMEL SAUCE:

2 tablespoons butter	Salt to taste
2 tablespoons flour	Dash of white pepper
1 cup warm milk	Dash of nutmeg

Melt butter over moderate heat and add flour, stirring until well blended. Cook a few seconds until mixture is bubbly. Remove from heat. Stir in warm milk, two tablespoons at a time until you have used one-half cup. Blend well. Return to low heat and add remaining milk slowly, stirring constantly until thickened. Season with salt, pepper and nutmeg to taste. Makes one cup.

CONTINUED

CONTINUED

PREPARE TRIANGLES:

Filo is usually packaged in one-pound cartons. There are approximately 20-24 sheets of filo per pound. Each sheet measures approximately 13x17 inches.

Filo should be placed in refrigerator from freezer 2-4 hours before using or left at room temperature for an hour to thaw for handling. When ready to use, unroll filo and cover with foil or wax paper and top with a damp towel to prevent filo from drying. Pin towel to foil at one end so they can be lifted together when getting sheets of filo.

Melt the half-pound sweet butter. Place one sheet of filo lengthwise on a cutting board. Brush with butter. Top with second sheet of filo and brush with butter. With pastry cutter, divide filo equally into six strips (each strip will be approximately 2x13 inches). Place full teaspoon of crab mixture in bottom corner of one strip. Fold pastry over in triangular shape, folding over and over to end of strip. Brush triangle with butter. Prick with a toothpick. Place on baking sheet, seam side down. Bake 15-20 minutes or until golden. Makes approximately 30 triangles. Delicious as an hors d'oeuvre!

Southeastern Wildlife Cookbook

Seafood Casserole

2/3 cup rice	1 pound crabmeat
1 pound shrimp	1 cup English peas
1/2 teaspoon curry powder	3 tablespoons chopped onion
1 teaspoon Worcestershire	1/2 cup chopped green pepper
3/4 teaspoon salt	1 cup chopped celery
1/8 teaspoon pepper	1 cup buttered bread crumbs
1 cup mayonnaise	

Cook rice and drain. Cook shrimp and cut lengthwise. Combine rice and shrimp with curry powder, Worcestershire, salt, pepper, mayonnaise and mix all together. Add crabmeat, drained English peas, onion, green pepper and celery. Toss together well and place in 2-quart casserole. Top with buttered bread crumbs. Bake at 350° for 45 minutes. Serves 6.

Carolina Cuisine

Meats

A pit crew hustles on the Darlington Speedway. Each September The Labor Day 500 is held here. It is called the "Granddaddy of all stock car racing."

Roast Loin of Veal with Lowcountry Sauce

1 (2 1/2-pound) veal loin

Brown the loin of veal in oil, in hot, heavy skillet. (Just brown lightly for a couple of minutes on both sides.)

Remove loin to rack over roasting pan and season with salt and pepper. Roast 375° for 25-30 minutes.

SAUCE:

2 pounds mushrooms	**1 tablespoon flour**
1/2 cup butter	**1 teaspoon salt**
2 tablespoons chopped shallots	**1/2 teaspoon freshly cracked white pepper**
Juice of one-half lemon	**2 cups heavy cream**
1/4 cup dry Madeira wine or dry sherry	

Roughly chop mushrooms. Heat butter in heavy skillet over medium high heat and cook shallots for 3 minutes stirring. Do not let them brown. Add chopped mushrooms and lemon juice. Cook, stirring until mixture looks dry. Add Madeira wine and cook until it evaporates. Sprinkle flour, salt, and pepper over mushrooms and stir in. Add heavy cream and continue cooking until sauce is thickened.

To serve: Slice loin thin and arrange on pretty platter. Generously ladle on mushroom sauce. Sprinkle with some chopped fresh parsley. Serves 4.

Charleston Receipts Repeats

Veal Parmigiana

1 pound veal cutlets
1 egg, slightly beaten
1/2 cup fine dry bread
  crumbs
2 tablespoons salad oil
1 (10 3/4-ounce) can tomato
  soup
1/4 cup water

1/4 cup minced onion
1 clove garlic, crushed
1/8 teaspoon thyme
8 mushrooms, sliced
4 ounces mozzarella cheese,
  grated
2 tablespoons freshly grated
  Parmesan cheese

Dip veal in egg, then in bread crumbs, and fry in salad oil until brown on each side. Place veal in a shallow baking dish, 12 x 7 1/2 x 2-inch. Blend soup, water, onion, garlic and thyme. Pour over meat. Top with mushroom slices, mozzarella cheese and sprinkle with Parmesan cheese. Bake in a 350° oven, about 30 minutes or until hot and bubbling. Serves 4.

A Taste of South Carolina

Medallions of Veal and Shrimp with a Grape Dijon Sauce

12 medium shrimp
4 (4-ounce) slices
  scaloppini veal
1/4 cup flour
1 tablespoon butter
2 tablespoons brandy
  (optional)

3 cups heavy cream
3 - 4 tablespoons Dijon
  mustard
1/2 pound red and white
  seedless grapes

Peel and devein shrimp and set aside.

Cut veal slices in half to make eight pieces, tenderize with meat mallet, then flour both sides. Melt butter in skillet on high. Add veal and shrimp; when edges turn brown, turn over, add brandy and flame. When flame goes out, add heavy cream and simmer on low for 2-3 minutes. Add mustard and stir occasionally until mixture thickens. Salt and pepper to taste. Add grapes and serve. Makes 4 servings.

Note: When flaming, be sure to stand back from skillet; flame will dissipate quickly.

One Course At A Time

Marinated Beef Tenderloin

1 cup catsup
2 teaspoons prepared
  mustard
1 teaspoon Worcestershire
  sauce
1 1/2 cups water
2 (.07-ounce) packs Italian
  salad dressing

1 beef tenderloin, trimmed
  (4 to 6-pounds)
Watercress, optional
Red and green grapes,
  optional

Combine catsup, mustard, Worcestershire, water and salad dressing. Mix well. Spear meat in several places and place in zip top bag. Pour marinade in bag and seal tightly. Place bag in shallow pan and refrigerate 8 hours, turning occasionally. Drain off and reserve marinade. Place tenderloin on a rack in baking dish. Insert meat thermometer. Bake at 425° for 30-45 minutes or until 140° for rare. Bake until 150° registers for medium rare and 160° for medium. Baste occasionally with marinade while baking. Remove to serving platter and garnish with watercress and grapes if desired. Serve remaining marinade with meat. Yields 12 servings. A Christmas specialty.

One Course At A Time

Bachelor's Roast

1 (4-pound) beef roast
Salt and pepper
Garlic salt

3 tablespoons cooking oil
1 small bottle Coca-Cola
1 (14-ounce) bottle catsup

Score roast in several places, fill each place with 1/2 teaspoon each of salt, pepper and garlic salt. Sear roast on all sides on oil. Remove from pan, pour off excess fat. Place roast in foil-lined roasting pan. Pour Coca-cola and catsup over roast. Cover loosely with foil and bake for 3 hours at 325°.

Cooking...Done the Baptist Way

Marinated Chuck Roast

3 pound chuck roast (1 1/2
  to 2-inches thick)
1 teaspoon monosodium
  glutamate
1/3 cup wine vinegar
2 tablespoons cooking oil
1 teaspoon prepared mustard

1/4 teaspoon pepper
1/4 cup catsup
2 tablespoons soy sauce
1 tablespoon Worcestershire
  sauce
1 teaspoon salt
1/4 teaspoon garlic powder

Sprinkle both sides of the roast with MSG. Place it in a shallow baking dish. Combine the other ingredients over medium heat. Pour this marinade over the roast and marinate at least 2-3 hours, turning once or twice. Grill over hot coals about 6 inches from the coals. Turn and baste with marinade every 10-15 minutes. Cook 45 minutes to 1 hour for medium roast.

Bethel Food Bazaar II

Swiss Steak Royal

2 pounds round steak, cut
  1-inch thick
3/4 cup flour
2 cups sliced onion
2 tablespoons fat
1 clove garlic, finely
  chopped

1/2 cup chili sauce or
  canned tomatoes
1 teaspoon dry mustard
2 teaspoons salt
1/4 teaspoon pepper
1/2 cup water

Pound flour into steak with a meat hammer or edge of heavy saucer. Lightly pan-fry onions in a hot fat in a skillet. Remove from pan. Brown steak on both sides. Cover with onions. Mix remaining ingredients and pour over steak. Cover. Cook over low heat or bake in moderate oven, 350°, about 1 1/2 hours, or until fork tender. Makes 6 servings.

The South Carolina Cook Book

Smothered Steak Daufuskie Style

Steak—any kind and any
  amount
Raw potatoes—enough
  sliced to cover steak

Onions—enough sliced to
  cover potatoes
Salt and pepper to taste

Salt, pepper, and flour favorite steak and brown in a little oil in skillet. Take steak up and remove most of grease from pan. At this point, a little brown gravy may be made, then put the steak in gravy (or just put steak back into pan). Cover steak with sliced Irish potatoes and top with sliced onions. A shake of salt and pepper over the whole thing and maybe a dash of soy sauce improves the flavor. Cover and simmer until all is done.

A delicious and quick one-dish-meal.

Stirrin' The Pots On Daufuskie

Beef Burgundy

1 1/2 pounds round steak	1 bay leaf
Flour	1 can sliced mushrooms
Salt and pepper	Instant parsley
Cooking oil	Powdered garlic
2 cups water	1 cup burgundy wine
1 onion, chopped	

Cut steak into large cubes and shake well in a bag with flour, salt and pepper. Brown in oil along with onion. Add about 2 cups water and 1 bay leaf. Steam for 1 hour. Then add mushrooms, pinch of parsley, pinch of garlic, and a cup of burgundy wine. Simmer until mushrooms are tender and remove bay leaf. Serve over hot rice. Serves 6.

The Sandlapper Cookbook

Chinese Pepper Steak

1 pound sirloin steak	1/2 cup beef broth
2 tablespoons margarine	(1 beef bouillon cube to
2 tablespoons chopped	1/2 cup hot water)
onion	1/2 teaspoon salt
1 clove garlic, minced	Pepper to taste
1 cup chopped celery	2 tablespoons cornstarch
2 green peppers, cut in	2 tablespoons cold water
strips	1 tablespoon soy sauce

Put beef in freezer until partially frozen. Slice into thin strips. Heat margarine in large skillet. Add beef and brown. Add onions, garlic, celery and green pepper. Sauté until onions and pepper are tender but not browned. Add broth, salt and pepper. Cover and simmer 20 minutes or until beef is tender. Blend cornstarch with water and soy sauce until smooth. Gradually add to mixture of beef and vegetables and simmer 3 minutes. Serve hot over cooked rice. Serves 4.

Culinary Crinkles

Beef Stew

1 pound stew beef	1 package frozen snapbeans
1 package short ribs of beef	1 can tomatoes
3 large onions, chopped	1/2 box macaroni shells (or
3 stalks celery, chopped	4 potatoes cubed)
1 package frozen butter-	Bay leaf
beans	Salt to taste
1 package frozen corn	Pepper to taste

In large pot of water, boil meat, onions and celery for 30 minutes.
Add other ingredients (except the shells)...simmer for 2 or 3 hours.
Remove bones, add shells and simmer 30 minutes longer. Delicious over rice, alone, or with cornbread. Better next day; good
all week.

Stirrin' The Pots On Daufuskie

Crock Pot Barbecued Beef Stew

2 pounds stew beef	1/3 cup barbecue sauce
2 tablespoons oil	2 cups beef stock
1 cup sliced onions	1/2 teaspoon salt
1 large clove garlic	1 (4-ounce) can mushrooms
1/2 cup bell pepper	3 tablespoons cornstarch
1/8 teaspoon pepper	1/4 cup cold water
1 (8-ounce) can tomatoes	

Brown beef in oil. Put sliced onions, garlic and pepper in bottom of crock pot. Add the beef and remaining ingredients except the cornstarch and water. Cook on low 8-10 hours. Dissolve cornstarch in water; add to crock pot, and simmer until
thick. Serve over rice.

Carolina Cuisine Encore!

 Columbia is the boyhood home of President Woodrow Wilson. The
house was built in 1872. The century old garden originally planted
by Mrs. Wilson can still be enjoyed today.

French Oven Beef Stew

2 pounds stew beef, cubed	1 tablespoon sugar
2 medium onions, sliced thin	1 tablespoon salt
3 stalks celery, sliced	1/4 teaspoon pepper
4 medium carrots, sliced	1/2 teaspoon basil
1 cup tomato juice	2 or 3 potatoes, cubed in
1/3 cup tapioca	medium pieces

Combine all but potatoes in a 2 1/2-quart casserole. Cover. Bake at 325° for 3 1/2 hours. Put potatoes in last hour. Stir occasionally.

Note: Excellent!

Thoroughbred Fare

Porcupine Beef Balls

MIX AND SHAPE IN RATHER FIRM BALLS:

1 pound ground beef

1 teaspoon salt

1/2 cup washed, uncooked
rice

SAUTÉ IN 2 TABLESPOONS BUTTER FOR 3 MINUTES:

2 tablespoons green pepper,
chopped

1/2 cup chopped celery

2 tablespoons chopped onion

2 cups tomato purée

As the meat balls are shaped, place in greased baking dish.
Mix chopped vegetables and purée and pour over meat balls.
Bake uncovered so the rice will steam—350° about 1 1/2 hours.
During the last 15 minutes, the dish may be uncovered so the
meat will brown. Garnish with sprigs of parsley and fan-shaped
pieces of pickle. Serves 8.

The South Carolina Cook Book

Old Fashioned Beef Pie with Herb Crust

2 pounds boneless beef
  chunks (such as bottom
  round or lean chuck)
3 tablespoons flour
2 1/2 teaspoons salt,
  divided
1/8 teaspoon pepper
2 tablespoons shortening
1/2 teaspoon thyme, divided
1/2 cup red wine (burgundy)
1 1/4 cups water, divided
1/2 bay leaf

1 teaspoon Worcestershire
  sauce
2 cups cubed potatoes
4 large carrots cut in
  1-inch slices
1/2 cup celery cut in 1-inch
  slices
8 small white onions, peeled
1 double pie crust to fit
  10x10-inch casserole
1/4 teaspoon marjoram
1 tablespoon butter

Cut beef into 1 1/4-inch cubes; roll in mixture of flour, 1 1/2 teaspoons of salt and 1/8 teaspoon of pepper. Brown cubes in hot shortening and sprinkle remaining flour and 1/4 teaspoon thyme over meat. Add wine, 1/2 cup water, bay leaf and Worcestershire sauce. Heat to simmering stage and cover. Cook slowly until tender, about 1 1/2 hours. Add vegetables, 1/2 cup water and remaining 1 teaspoon salt. Cover; cook slowly until vegetables are tender, about 30 minutes. Prepare crust while vegetables are cooking. Blend pie crust, 1/4 teaspoon thyme and 1/4 teaspoon marjoram. Add remaining 1/4 cup water. Roll to fit 10x10x3-inch casserole. Put meat mixture in casserole and top with crust, tucking in edges. Prick crust. Brush with melted butter. Bake 25-30 minutes at 400°. Serves 6-8.

Carolina Cuisine Encore!

 South Carolinians led the resistance to the Stamp Act, and more Revolutionary battles were fought in this state than in any other.

Meat Loaf

1 1/2 pounds ground beef
1 cup Rice Krispies
1 small onion, chopped
1/2 (8-ounce) can tomato
  sauce

1 egg, beaten
Dash pepper
1 teaspoon salt

Mix well and form into loaf. Place in baking dish. Mix all the sauce ingredients and pour over loaf in dish. Bake at 325° for 1 1/4 hours, uncovered. Serves 6.

SAUCE:
1/2 (8-ounce) can tomato
  sauce
2 tablespoons brown sugar
2 tablespoons prepared
  mustard

2 tablespoons vinegar
1 cup water

Strictly For Boys

Cheeseburger Pie

2 pounds hamburger
1 cup onions, chopped
3 eggs
1 1/2 cups milk

1 cup Bisquick
1 pint pizza sauce
2 cups mozzarella cheese,
  shredded

In a saucepan, brown hamburger and onions. Season slightly. Drain and pour in a loaf pan. Mix eggs, milk, Bisquick and pour over hamburger mixture. Pour pizza sauce on and top with cheese. Bake at 350° for 30-40 minutes.

500 Favorite Recipes

Cheese Stuffed Meatloaf

1/2 pound mozzarella cheese	1/2 teaspoon salt
2 pounds lean ground beef	1 teaspoon oregano
2 eggs	Dash of pepper
1/2 cup packaged seasoned	2 medium onions, minced
bread crumbs	8 paper thin, boiled ham
1 cup tomato juice	slices

Grate cheese; set aside. Combine beef, eggs, bread crumbs, tomato juice, salt, oregano and pepper. Sauté onions in a little vegetable oil until golden brown. Add to meat mixture. Mix well. Turn out on sheet of aluminum foil. Flatten into oblong about 1-inch thick. Place ham slices on meat, keeping about 1 inch from edge. Sprinkle grated cheese on ham. Use the foil to fold meat mixture over ham and cheese, closing all openings. Turn loaf from foil into a greased long pan (8x5x3-inches). Pat with fingers to fill corners of pan and shape loaf, which will completely fill pan and be rounded slightly on top. Bake at 325° for 60-75 minutes, depending on degree of rareness desired. Very delicious and good for freezing

Olivia's Favorite Menus and Recipes

Mexican Casserole

1 pound ground lean beef
1 tablespoon cooking oil
1 (15-ounce) can Mexican
  pinto beans
1 (10-ounce) can tomato
  sauce

1 cup shredded sharp cheese
1 tablespoon minced onion
1 (6-ounce) package corn
  chips (set aside 1 cup)

Put beef and cooking oil in saucepan and brown meat; drain. Mix with remaining ingredients and put into a 2 1/2-quart casserole. Bake at 375° for 30 minutes, then add topping.

TOPPING:

1 cup sour cream   1/2 cup shredded cheese

Do not mix the two ingredients together. Spread sour cream on first, then sprinkle cheese alternately with the 1 cup corn chips which was set aside. Bake 10 minutes longer, uncovered.

   Note: Freezes well, but leave off sour cream until ready to use.

Olivia's Favorite Menus and Recipes

Chili Con Carne
(with tomatoes)

1 pound ground beef
2 medium onions (about 1 cup)
1 cup chopped green pepper
1 (16-ounce) can tomatoes
1 cup catsup
1 or 2 teaspoons chili powder

1 teaspoon salt
1/8 teaspoon red pepper (optional)
1/8 teaspoon paprika (optional)
1 (15 1/2-ounce) can kidney beans, drained

Cook and stir beef, onion and green pepper in a large skillet until meat is brown and onion is tender. Drain off fat. Stir in remaining ingredients except kidney beans. Heat to boiling. Reduce heat; cover and simmer 2 hours. Stir occasionally. (May cook uncovered 45 minutes.) Stir in beans; heat. Makes 4 or 5 (1 cup) servings.

Cooking...Done the Baptist Way

Stuffed Cabbage

2 onions (chopped)
2 pounds ground beef
1 cabbage
1 small box minute rice
1 (#2) can tomatoes

Salt and pepper
1 teaspoon sugar
1/2 cup catsup
1 cup sherry

Sauté onions in saucepan. Add ground beef and cook until grayed. Place 12 cabbage leaves in boiling, salted water until wilted. Place in flat casserole dish and fill with meat mixture. Fold over cabbage leaves and secure with toothpicks. Sprinkle rice over cabbage leaves. Combine tomatoes, salt, pepper, sugar, catsup, and sherry. Pour over cabbage and rice and cook at 350° until rice is done.

The Sandlapper Cookbook

Lasagne á la Mama

4 ounces lean beef	Salt
4 ounces lean pork	Freshly ground black pepper
1 slice mortadella (Italian	1/2 cup red wine
bologna)*	1 cup tomato sauce
1 slice cooked ham	1 cup ricotta cheese
1 stick celery	Nutmeg
1 small carrot	1 tablespoon milk
1 medium onion	1 pound fresh spinach
1/4 cup butter	lasagne
Virgin olive oil	Fresh Reggiano Parmesan
3 cloves garlic, chopped	cheese, grated

Chop the beef, pork, mortadella and cooked ham together with the celery, carrot and onion.

Cook all the ingredients in a saucepan with butter, oil and garlic. Season with salt and pepper. When browned, pour in the wine. Allow wine to evaporate.

Add the tomato sauce (or the equivalent amount of fresh Italian tomatoes, sieved). Simmer until the meats are cooked and the sauce is thick.

Beat the ricotta in a bowl, season with salt and pepper and nutmeg. Add the milk.

Cook the lasagne noodles a few at a time until they are just softened, then remove and place on a cloth to drain.

Prepare a baking dish with some softened butter. Spread a thin layer of the sauce on the bottom. Spoon in some of the meat mixture. Cover with a layer of noodles, making them touch. Do not overlap the noodles. Follow with a layer of cheese and more noodles and finally another cheese layer finishing with a top layer of noodles. Pour some melted butter over the final layer.

Bake at 350-375° oven for 20-25 minutes or until the top layer of noodles are golden.

Serve immediately. Pass the Parmesan with a grater.

*Available sometimes in gourmet specialty shops or deli. However if unavailable, you may omit.

One Course At A Time

Popover Mushroom Pizza Bake

BASE:

1 pound ground beef
1 pound fresh mushrooms or
 1 (8-ounce) can mushrooms
1/2 cup chopped green
 pepper
1/2 cup chopped onion

1 (10 1/2-ounce) can or jar
 pizza sauce with cheese
1 teaspoon oregano
1 teaspoon garlic salt

POPOVER TOP:

2 eggs
1 cup milk
1 tablespoon vegetable oil
1 cup all-purpose flour
Salt to taste

1/2 cup grated Parmesan
 cheese
1 1/2 cups (6 ounces)
 shredded mozzarella cheese

Preheat oven to 400°. Prepare base. In large skillet or Dutch oven, cook and stir ground beef, mushrooms, green pepper and onion until meat is browned. Thoroughly drain fat. Stir in pizza sauce, oregano and garlic salt. Simmer 10 minutes.

Meanwhile, prepare Popover Top. In small bowl of electric mixer, blend together eggs, milk and oil. Add flour and salt. Beat at medium speed about 1 1/2 minutes or until smooth. Spoon hot beef mixture into shallow 2-quart baking dish. Sprinkle with mozzarella cheese. Pour topping evenly over base. Sprinkle with Parmesan cheese. Bake about 30 minutes or until puffy and golden brown. Makes 6-8 servings.

Bethel Food Bazaar II

Reuben Quiche

1 (9-inch) deep dish frozen
  pie shell
1 (10-ounce) can sauerkraut,
  well drained
1 tablespoon caraway seeds
4 tablespoons butter
1 1/2 (2.5-ounce) packages
  corned beef, chopped
1 (4-ounce) package Swiss
  cheese, shredded

1 whole egg
2 egg yolks
1 cup half-and-half
1/4 teaspoon dry mustard
1 teaspoon instant minced
  onion
Salt and pepper to taste

Defrost pie shell; prick and bake 10 minutes at 425°. Press
sauerkraut firmly between hands to be sure it is well drained.
Sauté sauerkraut and caraway seeds in butter for 3-4 minutes. Chop the corned beef, shred the cheese, but do not mix.
Preparation to this point can be done the day before. When
ready to bake, beat the egg, egg yolks, half-and-half, mustard,
onion, salt and pepper until smooth. To assemble the quiche,
layer the sauerkraut, corned beef and Swiss cheese in baked
pie shell; then pour the egg mixture over all. Bake at 350° for
about 40 minutes, or until set. Yield: 6 servings.

Prescriptions for Good Eating

Roast Pork Au Vin Blanc

1 (5-pound) pork loin roast	1/3 cup dry white wine
1/2 large lemon	3/4 cup sour cream
1 garlic clove, halved	Pineapple slices
Marjoram	Fresh peeled oranges
Salt and pepper to taste	Fresh parsley sprigs

Rub pork roast with lemon, garlic clove and marjoram. Sprinkle with salt and pepper. Place seasoned pork loin in roaster and cook, uncovered, in 325° oven for 2 1/2 - 3 hours or until meat thermometer registers 185°. Remove roast from pan and keep warm. To make gravy, heat wine in pan juices. Stir in sour cream and season with salt and pepper. Serve gravy with pork loin. Garnish roast with pineapple slices, oranges and parsley sprigs.

Uptown Down South

Spiced Pineapple Pork Roast

1 (4-pound) pork loin roast	1 teaspoon prepared mustard
1 (12-ounce) jar pineapple	1/4 teaspoon salt
preserves	1/4 teaspoon cinnamon
2 tablespoons honey	1/4 teaspoon ground cloves
2 tablespoons red wine	1 (8-ounce) can pineapple
vinegar	slices, drained

Place roast in shallow roasting pan. Insert meat thermometer into thickest part of roast, not touching bone. Roast, uncovered, at 350° about 2 1/2 or 3 hours or until meat thermometer registers 170°. Combine pineapple preserves, honey, vinegar, mustard, salt, cinnamon and cloves in a small saucepan. During last 20 minutes of roasting time, garnish roast with pineapple slices and brush with pineapple glaze several times. Serve remaining glaze warm with roast. Yield: 6 servings.

Bethel Food Bazaar II

24 Hour Crockpot Barbecue

2 medium onions
4 - 5 pound Boston butt pork
  roast
2 cups water
6 cloves

1 onion, chopped
1 (16-ounce) bottle hickory
  smoked barbecue sauce
10 drips Tabasco pepper
  sauce

The night before serving, put 1 sliced onion in crockpot. Add meat, water and cloves. Top with 1 sliced onion. Cover and cook on low 10-12 hours, or until meat falls off bone. Drain contents of crockpot in colander. Remove bone and fat from meat. Discard onions and cloves. Return meat to crockpot. Add chopped onion, barbecue sauce and Tabasco pepper sauce. Cover and cook remainder of day on low, or 1-3 hours on high. Serve on warm buns. Yield: 6-8 servings.

Note: Leftovers will freeze. Good with coleslaw and corn on the cob.

Prescriptions for Good Eating

Baked Pork Chops with Potatoes

4 (3/4-inch) lean pork chops
1 teaspoon salt
1/2 teaspoon pepper
4 thinly sliced, pared
  potatoes

1/2 cup minced onion
1/2 cup milk
1 can cream of mushroom
  soup

Place chops in a 13x9x2-inch baking pan. Sprinkle with half of the salt and pepper. Mix potatoes and onions together; place over chops. Sprinkle with remaining salt and pepper. Gradually add milk to mushroom soup. Stir until smooth. Pour over potatoes; cover. Bake in preheated oven at 350° for 1 hour. Makes 4 servings.

Chops may be browned before placing in baking dish.

Olivia's Favorite Menus and Recipes

Oven-Cooked Spareribs

3 pounds lean pork spareribs
1 cup catsup
1 tablespoon dry mustard
4 tablespoons brown sugar
1 teaspoon nutmeg
1 teaspoon allspice
1/2 teaspoon cinnamon
1 teaspoon salt
1 teaspoon white pepper
1 small onion chopped and
  browned in a tablespoon of
  margarine

Trim and cut spareribs into serving pieces. Wash, pat dry. Lightly salt and pepper. Put into covered roasting pan. Cook for 1 hour at 300°. Drain after 1 hour and add sauce of the above listed ingredients. Coat each piece, turn over after half hour and coat the other side. Cook for another 1/2 hour. Total cooking time, 2 hours. Serves 4.

The Sandlapper Cookbook

Busy Day Chops

1/4 cup butter or margarine
1 cup rice, uncooked
1 (10 1/2-ounce) can French
  onion soup
1 (10 1/2-ounce) can beef
  broth
4-6 pork chops

Melt butter in a frying pan, add rice and stir constantly over low heat until brown. Transfer to a 2 1/2-quart casserole, add soup and broth and top with pork chops. Cover and bake at 350° for 1 1/2 hours. Pork chops will be tender and flavorful! Serves 4-6. For variety, add bell pepper, celery and mushrooms.

Stir Crazy!

 Branchville hosts a September Raylrode Daze Festival to celebrate the town's title as "the country's oldest railroad junction."

Sweet-Sour Pork

1 1/2 pounds lean pork, cut
  into strips 2 inches long
  and 1/2-inch wide
2 tablespoons fat
1/4 cup water
1/4 cup brown sugar
2 tablespoons cornstarch
1/2 teaspoon salt
1/4 - 1/3 cup vinegar

1 cup pineapple juice
1 tablespoon soy sauce
3/4 cup green pepper, cut in
  strips
1/4 cup onions, thinly
  sliced
1 (#2) can pineapple chunks
1/3 cup sweet pickles, cut up
Pickle juice

Brown pork slightly in hot fat. Add water, cover and cook slowly 1 hour. Combine brown sugar, cornstarch, salt, vinegar, pineapple juice and soy sauce. Mix. Cook until slightly thick, stirring constantly. Pour over cooked pork; let stand 10 minutes. Add green pepper, onions and pineapple chunks and heat only 3-5 minutes. Add sweet pickles and a little juice. Vegetables should remain crisp. Serve with rice or cooked buttered noodles. Serves 6. Recipe can be doubled or tripled.

Southern Cooking

Mushroom Baked Ham

1 teaspoon dry mustard
1/2 teaspoon ginger
1/2 cup dry white wine

1 (1 1/2-inch thick)
  center slice ham

Mix together and pour over one 1 1/2-inch thick center slice of ham. Marinate for several hours. Reserve marinade. Drain ham, brown in a small amount of fat. Add a little water and place in 325° oven to cook for about an hour.

SAUCE:
1 medium sized minced
  onion
3 tablespoons margarine
1/4 cup flour

1 cup milk
1 (4 1/2-ounce) can
  mushrooms

CONTINUED

CONTINUED

Sauté onion in margarine and push to side. Add flour and stir; slowly add milk and mushroom liquid. Heat stirring until smooth and thick. Add mushrooms and reserved marinade. Pour sauce over ham. Bake until bubbly at 350° (about 20 minutes). May be prepared ahead and frozen. Serves 8.

Carolina Cuisine

Pawleys Island Ham

1 (12 - 14-pound) smoked
  ham (processed, pre-
  cooked variety)
3/4 cup bourbon

2 cups dark brown sugar
1 tablespoon dry mustard
Cloves

Preheat the oven to 325°. Place the ham fat side up on a rack set in a shallow roasting pan. Bake without basting for 20-25 minutes per pound or until done. When the ham is cool enough to handle, cut away the rind. Score the ham by cutting deeply through the fat until you reach the meat, making the incisions 1/2-inch apart lengthwise and crosswise. Brush the ham on all sides with 1/2 cup of the bourbon. Then combine the sugar, mustard, and remaining bourbon. Pat this mixture firmly into the scored fat. Stud the fat at each intersection or in the center of each diamond with a whole clove.

Baste lightly with drippings on the bottom of the pan and bake the ham undisturbed in 450° oven for 15-20 minutes or until the sugar has melted and formed a brilliant glaze. Garnish with pineapple slice, cherries, apricots, or mandarin orange slices. Save the bone for okra soup! Serves 28.

Calories 329.15, Protein 25.09gm, Fat 16.37gm, Carbohydrates 16.85gm, Fiber 0.00gm, Cholesterol 120.06mg, Saturated Fats 5.49gm, Iron 4.26mg, Calcium 28.86mg, Sodium 1513.49mg, Potassium 522.14mg, Vitamin A 0.00 I.U., Vitamin C 0.00mg, Thiamine 0.73mg, Riboflavin 0.27mg, Niacin 5.25mg

The Enlightened Gourmet

Sausage and Rice Casserole

1 pound hot sausage,
  browned and drained
1 cup celery, chopped
1 cup onion, chopped
1 cup bell pepper, chopped

1 cup rice, uncooked
1 (14 1/2-ounce) can chicken
  broth, combined with water
  to yield 2 cups liquid
Salt and pepper to taste

Combine all ingredients in a 2-quart casserole. Cover and bake at 325° for 1 hour. Serves 6. Two cups raw shrimp may be substituted for sausage.

Stir Crazy!

Pork and Beans with Sausage Casserole

1 pound pork sausage
2 apples, peeled and diced
  (dice small)

1 large onion, chopped fine
2 large cans pork and beans,
  drained (Campbell's)

Brown and crumble sausage; drain. Dice apples and onion. Combine all ingredients. Mix well and pour mixture into a greased baking dish (13x9x2 inches). Bake until bubbly.

Tip: A good dish for a picnic.

Olivia's Favorite Menus and Recipes

 Of the many museums throughout the state, the magnificent new State Museum in Columbia shows off art, history and technology in an 80,000-square-foot converted textile mill.

Ham and Cheese Noodle Casserole

1 (8-ounce) package wide
  noodles
2 1/2 cups or 3/4 pound
  cooked ham, diced
2 cups or 8 ounces shredded
  Swiss cheese

1/3 cup green pepper,
  chopped
2 tablespoons onion, chopped
1 teaspoon salt
1 cup sour cream

Cook noodles according to package directions; drain. Toss together noodles, ham, cheese, green pepper, onions, and salt in large bowl. Blend in sour cream. Turn into 2-quart casserole. Bake at 375° for 25-30 minutes or until cheese melts and casserole is heated through. Top with green pepper rings. Serves 6.

Culinary Crinkles

Grilled Minted Leg of Lamb

1 cup dry white wine
1/4 cup fresh mint, finely
  chopped or 2 teaspoons
  dried mint
2 cloves garlic, crushed

1 teaspoon salt
1/2 teaspoon freshly ground
  black pepper
1 (7 - 8 pound) butterflied
  leg of lamb

Combine wine, mint, garlic, salt and pepper in a large shallow glass or ceramic dish. Put in lamb and turn to coat. Cover the dish with plastic wrap and refrigerate 3 or 4 hours. Turn the lamb once during this time. Grill the lamb about 4 inches from medium hot coals for 15 minutes per side. Brush often with remaining marinade during grilling. Remove from grill and slice the lamb crosswise in 1/4-inch thick slices. Serves 8.

Sea Island Seasons

Poultry and Game

*Table Rock, in the South Carolina Mountains, overlooks a peaceful
mountain lake.*

Chicken Piccata

4 chicken breast halves,
  skinned and boned
1 egg
3 tablespoons lemon juice,
  divided
1/4 cup all-purpose flour
1/8 teaspoon garlic powder

Dash paprika
1/4 cup butter or
  margarine, melted
2 chicken bouillon cubes
  dissolved in 1/2 cup
  boiling water

Beat egg with 1 tablespoon lemon juice. Combine flour, garlic powder and paprika. Dip chicken in egg mixture, then in flour. Brown both sides of chicken in butter. Add bouillon and 2 tablespoons lemon juice to chicken. Cover and simmer 20 minutes or until tender. Serves 4.

An extraordinary dish made from ordinary ingredients. Freezes well.

Stir Crazy!

Chicken Divan Parisienne

6 single chicken breasts,
  boned
1/4 cup butter
1/4 cup flour
1 cup chicken broth
1 cup milk

2 tablespoons mayonnaise
1 teaspoon prepared mustard
2 packages cooked frozen
  asparagus

Cook chicken until tender in simmering salted water. In pan melt butter, stir in flour, gradually add broth and milk, stir until smooth, add cheese, mayonnaise, mustard. Arrange asparagus in oblong baking dish. Place chicken breasts on top, cover with cheese sauce, sprinkle with paprika and almonds. Bake at 325° for 30 minutes. Serves 6.

Culinary Crinkles

Cashew Chicken with Snow Peas

1/3 cup sherry	4 split chicken breasts
3 tablespoons water	1/2 pound fresh mushrooms
1 tablespoon cornstarch	6 green onions
1 tablespoon brown sugar	1/4 pound fresh snow peas
1 tablespoon soy sauce	2 tablespoons peanut oil
2 teaspoons minced fresh ginger root	3/4 cup cashew nuts

In a medium size bowl, combine the sherry, water, cornstarch, brown sugar, soy sauce, and ginger root, mixing well. Bone, skin and dice the chicken. Place chicken in the bowl and marinate in the mixture for at least 1 hour. Wipe the mushrooms with a damp cloth, trim stems and cut mushrooms into thin slices. Slice the green onions into 1-inch pieces. Trim the snow peas and remove the strings. Set aside.

Heat the oil in a large skillet or wok. Drain chicken, reserving marinade. Cook chicken in the oil over medium high heat for about 5 minutes, or until done. Add mushrooms and cook until tender, 3-4 minutes. Add the reserved marinade, green onions and snowpeas. Cook until sauce is thickened. Sprinkle with cashews. Makes 4 servings.

The Sandlappers' Salvation Cookbook

Teriyaki Chicken

3 pounds boneless chicken breast	1/2 cup liquid brown sugar
1/2 cup Worcestershire sauce	1/4 cup red wine vinegar
1/2 cup soy sauce	1 tablespoon dried onions
	Dash of garlic salt

Mix all ingredients except chicken. Place chicken in sauce mixture and marinate for 1 or 2 hours. Place chicken in 350° oven with a small amount of sauce and bake for 35-40 minutes.

Thoroughbred Fare

Chicken Divan
(Microwave)

2 bunches fresh broccoli
1/4 cup water
1/2 teaspoon salt
4 chicken breasts
Salt and pepper
2 medium onions, sliced
1 can cream of chicken soup
1/4 cup sherry

2 tablespoons lemon juice
2 tablespoons Worcestershire
  sauce
Dashes of garlic powder,
  nutmeg, and curry powder
1/4 cup half and half
1/4 cup sour cream
1/2 cup Parmesan cheese

Cook broccoli for 12-14 minutes on High with 1/4 cup water and 1/2 teaspoon salt, covered, stirring once. Salt and pepper chicken breasts and cook 10-15 minutes on high, turning once. Put broccoli on bottom of 9x13-inch casserole, or one that fits in your microwave oven. Put chicken breasts on top. Cover with onion rings. Mix next 10 ingredients and pour over top. Microwave on High for 5 minutes or until hot.

Carolina Cuisine Encore!

Chicken in Wine with Oranges

Absolutely superb!

24 chicken breasts, boned
Seasoned flour
1 1/2 sticks butter, melted
1 cup brandy
1 cup white wine
1 cup red wine
2 tablespoons crabapple
  jelly

2 chicken bouillon cubes
1 tablespoon tomato paste
2 (3-ounce) cans sliced
  mushrooms
1 large can pearl onions
2 (11-ounce) cans mandarin
  oranges

Dredge the chicken in seasoned flour and brown in butter. Remove to a baking dish when brown. Add the brandy to the pan, ignite it, and let the alcohol burn off. Stir in everything except the oranges, mix well, and pour over chicken. Bake at 300° for 1 1/4 hours. Stir in the oranges at the last. This is better done the day before serving. Serves 12-15.

Flavored With Tradition

Lynn's Special Chicken

6 chicken breast halves,
  skinned and boned
1/2 pound fresh mushrooms,
  sliced
2 tablespoons butter
1/2 pound Swiss cheese,
  grated
2 eggs, beaten

1 cup flour
1 teaspoon salt
1/2 teaspoon pepper
1/2 teaspoon paprika
1 cup Italian bread crumbs
1/4 cup grated Swiss cheese
Butter

Pound chicken breasts to 1/4-inch thickness. Sauté mushrooms in butter and mix with cheese. Place mixture on each chicken breast and fold in half. Secure with wooden toothpick. Place in freezer until firm, about 20 minutes. Dip in eggs, then in a mixture of flour, salt, pepper and paprika. Dip in a mixture of bread crumbs and Swiss cheese. Sauté in butter in a skillet until lightly browned on all sides. Place in a buttered shallow casserole dish and bake at 325° for 20-30 minutes. Do not overcook. Serves 4-6.

Putting On The Grits

Golden Chicken Nuggets

3 whole chicken breasts,
  skinned and boned
1/2 cup all-purpose flour
3/4 teaspoon salt

2 teaspoons sesame seeds
1 egg, slightly beaten
1/2 cup water
Hot vegetable oil

Cut chicken into 1 - 1 1/2-inch pieces. Set aside. Combine the next five ingredients. Dip chicken into batter and fry in hot oil (375°) until golden brown. Drain on paper towels. Yield: 6-8 servings.

Thoroughbred Fare

Michael's Marvelous Chicken

Time well spent!

1 (8-ounce) carton sweet
  unsalted whipped butter
3 large scallions, chopped
  fine
6 mushrooms, chopped fine
1/2 pound white crab meat
1/4 pound shrimp
1/2 teaspoon ground basil
  leaves
1/4 teaspoon garlic
1/4 teaspoon poultry
  seasoning

1/2 lemon
Salt to taste
6-8 boned chicken breasts,
  pounded thin
1/2 cup white wine
Paprika and soft butter
1 scallion, chopped for
  sauce
4 mushrooms, sliced for
  sauce

Preheat oven to 350°. Mix butter, scallions, mushrooms, crab meat, and shrimp. Add spices, lemon juice and salt to taste. Place 2 tablespoons of mixture on each breast and fold corners to cover. Turn over and place in casserole. Pour white wine over, then dab each with butter and sprinkle with paprika. Bake for 15 minutes covered. Uncover and bake additional 10 minutes. To prepare sauce, pour liquid from casserole into small sauté pan and bring to boil. Add scallions and mushrooms and bring to boil again. Lower heat to simmer and reduce liquid to half.

Deglaze the sauce—stir in one tablespoon butter at a time (3 tablespoons total) with a whisk. Allow sauce to cool. Sauce can be spooned over each chicken breast. Serve with curried rice. Serves 6-8.

Charleston Receipts Repeats

Indian legend identifies Table Rock as the dinner table of a fabled giant chief. A nearby mountain called The Stool was said to be where he sat. Nearly 30 miles of trails wind through the state park in over 3,000 acres of green forest.

The Parson's Table Restaurant's Chicken Oskar

4 boneless chicken breasts	4 tablespoons butter
1 cup flour	2 tablespoons oil
1 teaspoon salt	8 asparagus spears, canned
1/2 teaspoon pepper	(or fresh asparagus,
1/2 teaspoon paprika	steamed)
2 - 3 eggs, beaten	6 ounces backfin crabmeat
Pinch of basil	Hollandaise sauce
1 cup Japanese or Italian	(commercial or homemade)
bread crumbs	

Flatten the chicken with a mallet on both sides. Dredge the chicken in flour seasoned with salt, pepper and paprika. Dip chicken in eggs. Mix basil into the bread crumbs and roll chicken in the mixture. In a large skillet, heat 2 tablespoons of the butter and all the oil. Sauté chicken until lightly browned. Remove and keep in warm oven. Heat asparagus and crabmeat in remaining butter over low heat until heated through. Put chicken on oven-proof plates and top with crabmeat and asparagus. Spoon hollandaise over top of each portion and place under broiler until light brown. Serves 4.

South Carolina's Historic Restaurants

Lemon Chicken

3 whole chicken breasts, split, skinned and boned
1/2 cup butter
1/4 cup dry vermouth or dry sherry
3 tablespoons lemon juice
2 tablespoons grated lemon rind
1 1/2 cups chicken broth
1 1/2 tablespoons flour
Salt and pepper
Grated Parmesan cheese
Sautéed mushrooms and/or cooked artichoke hearts

Sprinkle chicken breasts with salt and pepper. Melt butter in skillet and brown chicken on all sides. Sauté for 10 minutes or more until cooked through. Remove chicken to ovenproof platter. Add vermouth, lemon juice and rind to skillet. Stir and scrape pan drippings. Add broth. Blend flour and a little water; stir into broth. Stir constantly until slightly thickened. Pour over chicken, season, and sprinkle generously with cheese. Place pat of butter on top of each piece of chicken and brown under broiler. Add mushrooms and artichoke hearts. Yum!!!

The Museum Cookbook

Dandy Chicken

4 whole boneless chicken breasts, split in half for 8 pieces
Salt, pepper, paprika, garlic powder to taste
1 1/2 cups sour cream
2 tablespoons lemon juice
2 tablespoons Worcestershire sauce
1 package Pepperidge Farm herbed dressing mix
3/4 stick melted margarine

Sprinkle chicken breasts with salt, pepper, paprika, and garlic powder to taste. Mix sour cream, lemon juice and Worcestershire sauce. Dip each piece of chicken in sour cream mixture. Marinate at least 4 hours (or overnight). Roll in dressing mix and place in 9x13-inch baking dish. Drizzle with margarine. Bake at 325° for 1 hour and 15 minutes. Makes 8 servings.

Cooking...Done the Baptist Way

Spicy Baked Chicken Breasts

4 chicken breast halves, skinned
1 (8-ounce) can tomato sauce
1/3 cup barbeque sauce with honey
1/2 cup sliced fresh mushrooms

1 tablespoons Worcestershire sauce
1 teaspoon dried whole oregano
1 teaspoon seasoning blend
1 cup (4 ounces) shredded sharp Cheddar cheese

Placed chicken in a lightly greased baking dish. Combine remaining ingredients, except cheese, mixing well. Pour over chicken. Cover and bake at 350° for 50 minutes. Sprinkle chicken with cheese. Bake, uncovered, for an additional 2-3 minutes or until cheese is melted. Serve immediately.

Seasoned with Light

Hawaiian Chicken

1 (3-pound) broiler-fryer, cut up
1 teaspoon salt
1 cup flour
2 cups cooking oil

1 cup crushed pineapple
1 cup Kraft barbecue sauce
1 tablespoon cornstarch
1/2 teaspoon ground ginger

Wash and drain chicken, salt and let stand about 1 hour. Put flour in plastic bag, drop in chicken, 2 or 3 pieces at a time, shake well; continue until all chicken is floured. Heat cooking oil in heavy 10-inch frying pan. When oil is hot add the chicken and brown lightly on both sides, cook only long enough to brown. Place browned chicken in a 12 x 8 x 2-inch casserole. Mix pineapple, barbecue sauce, cornstarch and ginger. Spoon over browned chicken, cover tightly with foil and bake at 350° for 1 hour. Remove foil and return to oven for 10 minutes. Serves 6.

Strictly For Boys

Microwave Chicken Cacciatore

1 medium onion, chopped
1 medium green pepper, sliced
1 tablespoon butter
1 (28-ounce) can whole tomatoes
1/4 cup all-purpose flour
1 bay leaf
1 tablespoon dried parsley flakes
1 teaspoon salt
1 clove garlic, minced
1/2 teaspoon oregano
1 teaspoon paprika
1/4 teaspoon pepper
1/4 teaspoon basil
1/2 cup dry red wine, optional, or water
1 frying chicken, cut up (2 1/2 to 3 pounds)

In a 3-quart casserole combine onion, green pepper, and butter. Cover and cook on High for 4-5 minutes. Add tomatoes and flour; stir until smooth. Add remaining ingredients except chicken. Cover; cook on High 5 minutes. Add chicken pieces, immersing them in the sauce. Cover; cook on High 20-25 minutes until tender. Stir once during cooking. Allow to stand, covered, for 5 minutes. Remove bay leaf before serving.

Bethel Food Bazaar II

Barbecued Chicken

1/2 stick margarine or butter
2 1/2 cups water
1/2 cup vinegar
2 teaspoons dry mustard
2 teaspoons sugar
1/2 teaspoon onion salt
1/2 teaspoon garlic salt
2 1/2 teaspoons onions, chopped
1 teaspoon Tabasco
2 teaspoons black pepper
1 tablespoon salt
1 tablespoon Worcestershire sauce
1 tablespoon chili powder
2 chickens, quartered

Melt margarine in frying pan, add above ingredients except chicken and simmer 1/2 hour. Lay chicken pieces in roaster pan and butter well. Broil a minute or 2 on both sides. Then pour in part of sauce, basting well, later adding more sauce. Bake slowly, basting often in medium oven of 325° at least 2-3 hours until meat begins to pull away from bone.

Southern Cooking

Chicken in Wine Sauce for a Crowd

10 pieces of chicken
Flour
1 can cream of mushroom
  soup
1 cup white wine, preferably
  sherry
1/3 cup Worcestershire sauce

Seasonings to taste: Salt,
  pepper, garlic powder, onion
  powder, celery salt and
  paprika
Parmesan cheese (enough for
  liberal topping)

Flour chicken and arrange in large shallow baking pans in single layers. Mix all other ingredients except cheese. Pour evenly over chicken and sprinkle liberally with cheese.

Some additional paprika sprinkled over top also adds flavor and color. Bake at 350° 1 hour, or until chicken pieces are fork tender. This basic recipe serves 5 people allowing 2 pieces chicken each. Depending on your budget and ratio of children and adults, you can adjust recipe to serve any number. Fifty pieces of chicken will fit into 3 (12x15-inch) baking pans. Grease pans before adding chicken so that pieces can be removed more easily from pan.

Southern Cooking

Baked Chicken Parmesan

A make ahead, subtly seasoned dish. Serve a fresh vegetable salad with it.

1/2 cup salad oil
3 broiler-fryer chickens,
  cut in serving pieces
1 1/2 teaspoons oregano,
  divided
1 1/2 teaspoons salt,
  divided

Paprika
2 (4-ounce) cans sliced
  mushrooms
4 tablespoons grated
  Parmesan cheese

Line a 15x10x1-inch shallow pan with aluminum foil. Pour salad oil into pan. Place in a hot oven (425°) to heat, about 10 minutes. Remove pan from oven. Place chicken pieces, skin side down, in hot oil. Sprinkle with half the oregano and salt. Sprinkle lightly with paprika. Return to oven and bake 30 minutes. Turn chicken pieces. Sprinkle with remaining oregano, salt and lightly with paprika. Bake 15 minutes longer. Remove from oven. Spoon fat and drippings in pan over chicken. Pour mushrooms with liquid over chicken; sprinkle with Parmesan cheese. Bake 5 minutes longer. Good with rice. Makes 12 servings.

The Sandlapper's Salvation Cookbook

Curry Glazed Chicken

6 split chicken breasts (can be skinned)
6 chicken thighs (can be skinned)
6 chicken legs (can be skinned)
1 cut garlic clove
1/4 teaspoon salt
1/4 teaspoon pepper

1/2 lemon
1 stick butter or margarine
2 1/2 tablespoons curry powder
3/4 cup Dijon mustard
1 cup honey
1 teaspoon soy sauce
6 or 8 small green onions

Wipe chicken with paper towels and rub all over with cut clove of garlic. Season with salt and pepper. Squeeze lemon juice over chicken. Lay pieces one layer deep in large stove-to-table baking dish (or 2 dishes). Melt butter or margarine slowly and stir in curry powder. When heated through, stir in mustard, honey and soy sauce and pour over chicken. Cover with foil and refrigerate.

Warm to room temperature before cooking. Cook in a 350° oven for 1 hour until chicken is tender and richly glazed. Baste chicken occasionally with sauce. Decorate edge of dish with green onion plumes when you're ready to serve. Serve with saffron rice and condiments.

GREEN ONION PLUMES:
While chicken is baking, cut green onions into 1 1/2-inch pieces. Fringe each by making several cuts about 1/2-inch long all around each end. Dip in cold water, shake and chill in plastic bag.

SUGGESTED CURRY CONDIMENTS:
Chutney
Chopped peanuts
Raisins or currants
Pickles
Pineapple chunks
Mandarin oranges

Coconut
Chopped tomatoes
Chopped red or green pepper
Chopped candied ginger
Crisp bacon bits

Can be piled on saffron rice.

The Museum Cookbook

Chicken Pie

1/4 cup shortening
1/4 cup onion, chopped
1/4 cup flour
2 cups chicken stock
1/2 cup sliced cooked
  carrots

1/2 cup cooked peas
1/4 cup sliced cooked celery
1/2 cup chopped cooked onion
2 cups cubed cooked chicken

Melt shortening and sauté onion until tender and lightly browned. Remove half the onion to small bowl. Add flour to remaining onion and shortening; stir in well. Add chicken stock and cook, stirring constantly until thickened. Add carrots, peas, celery, onion and chicken; mix well. Pour into 2-quart baking dish. Top with Biscuit Topping and bake at 375° about 20 minutes, until biscuits are lightly browned. Serves 6.

BISCUIT TOPPING:
1/3 cup shortening
Reserved onions

1 1/2 cups self-rising flour
1/2 cup milk

Cut shortening and onions into flour. Add milk and stir until flour is just dampened. Press out on well floured surface and cut with biscuit cutter. Carefully lay biscuits on top of chicken mixture.

Strictly For Boys

Ham and Chicken Casserole

1/2 pound spaghetti (broken
  in 1-inch pieces and cooked
  until just tender)
2 - 3 cups diced chicken
1 cup diced ham
1/2 cup chopped pimento
1/2 cup green pepper,
  chopped

2 (10 3/4-ounce) cans cream
  of chicken soup
1 cup chicken broth
1/4 teaspoon celery salt
1/4 teaspoon pepper
1 large grated onion
2 cups grated cheese

Mix all but 1 cup cheese together and pour into 3-quart casserole. Add 1 extra cup of grated cheese to top of casserole. Bake at 350° for 1 hour. Serves 15.

A Taste of South Carolina

Savory Chicken Squares

3 ounces cream cheese
2 tablespoons margarine
2 cups cooked diced
   chicken or turkey
1/4 teaspoon salt
1/8 teaspoon pepper
2 tablespoons milk
1 tablespoon chopped onion
1 tablespoon pimento,
   chopped

1 (8-ounce) can Pillsbury
   crescent rolls
Melted butter
Italian bread crumbs
1 (10 3/4-ounce) can cream
   of chicken soup
Half-and-half

Blend cream cheese and margarine. Mix next six ingredients together. Separate crescent rolls. Form into rectangular shape by sealing the two rolls together. Roll dough a little to make thinner. Spoon 1/2 cup of the chicken mixture in the center of the dough. Bring the 4 corners together and pinch together to seal. Brush top with melted butter and sprinkle with Italian bread crumbs. Bake on greased baking sheet for 20-25 minutes at 350°.

Serve with cream sauce made with cream of chicken soup diluted with half-and-half. Use only enough half-and-half to make a cream sauce.

Olivia's Favorite Menus and Recipes

Chicken Party Pie Salad

Great for a summer luncheon, and so different!

1 (9-ounce) frozen pie shell
1 (3 - 3 1/2-pound) chicken
4 cups water
1 teaspoon salt
1 (9-ounce) can sliced
  pineapple
1 (3-ounce) can English
  walnuts, diced
1/2 cup diced celery

1 cup sour cream
2/3 cup mayonnaise
1/2 teaspoon salt
2 teaspoons lemon juice
1 tablespoon pineapple juice
Sharp Cheddar cheese,
  finely shredded
Sliced Spanish olives, for
  color

Bake pie shell according to directions on the package. Bring chicken, water and 1 teaspoon salt to boil in pan with a tight fitting lid. Reduce heat and simmer until tender. Cool in broth. When cooled, remove meat from bones, skin and cut into bite-size pieces. Drain pineapple, reserving 1 tablespoon juice, and cut into small bite-size pieces. Combine chicken, pineapple, walnuts and celery. In a separate bowl, combine the sour cream, mayonnaise, salt, lemon juice and pineapple juice. Add about a third of the sauce to the chicken mixture. Refrigerate both mixtures overnight. Just before serving, fill baked pie shell with the chicken salad, and ice the pie with the remaining sauce. Sprinkle with finely shredded cheese and put a row of sliced olives down the center of each piece of pie. Yield: 5 servings per pie, plus some chicken salad left over.

Note: Why not double the recipe to make 3 pies and have a luncheon?

Prescriptions for Good Eating

 The 1920s dance craze, the Big Apple, originated in Greater Columbia.

Hot Chicken Salad Casserole

4 cups cooked, cubed chicken or turkey	1/2 cup mayonnaise
2 cups celery	1 teaspoon salt
4 hard-boiled eggs	1/2 teaspoon Accent
2 tablespoons lemon juice	1 1/2 cups crushed, rippled potato chips
2/3 cup slivered almonds	3/4 cup grated Cheddar cheese
1 small jar chopped pimentos, drained	
3/4 cup sliced water chestnuts	

Mix all ingredients except chips and cheese together. Spread in an 8x8x2-inch casserole. Sprinkle top with crushed chips and grated cheese. Bake at 350° for 25 minutes. Do not over-bake!

Olivia's Favorite Menus and Recipes

Parmesan Picnic Chicken

1 1/2 cups bread crumbs	4 chicken breasts
3/4 teaspoon thyme	2 eggs
1 1/2 cups freshly grated Parmesan cheese	2 tablespoons water
Salt and pepper	1 tablespoon olive oil
	3 tablespoons butter

In a dish combine the bread crumbs, seasonings, and Parmesan. Salt and pepper lightly the four chicken breasts which have been cut into 16 pieces. Dip these pieces into the 2 eggs, lightly beaten with 2 tablespoons water. Coat with the bread crumbs. Adding as many chicken pieces as will fit in one layer, sauté in oil and butter for 3 minutes on each side or until well browned. Drain on brown paper. Wrap in foil for picnic. Do not refrigerate.

Bluffton's Favrite Recipes

Company Chicken 'n Beef

1 (6-ounce) jar chipped beef
1 whole fryer, cut up, or 4
  chicken breast halves
  (boneless breasts good for
  company)

Bacon slices
1 can cream of mushroom
  soup
1 (8-ounce) carton sour
  cream

Put chipped beef in bottom of lightly greased casserole dish. Place chicken pieces in next. Lay bacon slices on top of chicken. Bake uncovered for 30 minutes at 350°. Mix soup and sour cream together and pour over top. Bake 25-30 minutes more. (May want to cover loosely at this time.) The gravy is very good over rice.

Feeding the Faithful

Turkey Breast Cardinal

1 raw turkey breast
Flour
Salt and pepper
Butter and oil for frying
1 tablespoon Marsala,
  sauterne, or sherry

4 - 6 tablespoons chicken
  broth
6 thin slices prosciutto
1/2 pound mushrooms, sliced
  and sautéed
Parmesan cheese, grated

Skin turkey breast and carefully slice thinly into 6 fillets. Pound between wax paper and dredge in flour, salt and pepper. Cook slowly in butter and oil for about 5 minutes on each side. Have plenty to cook in but do not allow butter to burn. Add Marsala and chicken broth to pan, spooning liquid over turkey. Place a thin slice of prosciutto on each fillet, then a layer of sautéed mushroom slices. This much can be done ahead. Sprinkle with Parmesan cheese and heat until cheese melts and spreads. Serve immediately with pan juices spooned over top. Serves 6.

Sea Island Seasons

Duckling in Grape Juice Marinade

1 clove garlic, finely
   chopped
2 teaspoons salt
1 teaspoon marjoram
1 tablespoon chopped parsley
1/2 teaspoon caraway seed
1 teaspoon Kitchen Bouquet
3/4 cup grape juice
1/4 cup Madeira wine

1 (4-pound) duckling, cut
   into serving pieces
2 tablespoons butter
Parsley for garnish
Red and green grapes for
   garnish
1 (3-ounce) can sliced
   mushrooms, undrained
1 tablespoon cornstarch

In large bowl, combine garlic, salt, marjoram, parsley, caraway seed, Kitchen Bouquet, grape juice and wine. Marinate duck in mixture for 30 minutes. Melt butter in skillet over moderate heat. Remove meat from marinade and sauté until lightly brown on all sides; add marinade. Cover tightly and bake at 350° for 2 hours. Remove duck and place in serving dish. Garnish with wreaths of parsley and alternate bunches of red and green grapes. Blend mushrooms and cornstarch and add to juices, stirring constantly until sauce thickens. Serve sauce in separate bowl. Serves 2-3.

Putting On The Grits

Orange Barbecued Wild Duck or Goose

2 ducks or geese   1 onion
Vinegar   1 potato
Salt   Dash soy sauce

Clean ducks whole. After drawing, picking, singeing, and rinsing, put in milk cartons. Fill with warm water and freeze in block of ice. Thaw and soak ducks in milk solution of vinegar and salt water for 2 hours.

Peel and quarter onion and potato into pot of water. Add tablespoon salt and soy sauce. Bring to slow boil. Add ducks. Cover, boil slowly for 1 hour. Remove from pot, put into cold water to cool. Halve ducks lengthwise, wash each half. Dry with paper towel. Paint each half inside and out with barbecue sauce. Barbecue over medium hot coals. If ducks have been parboiled done, only a couple of minutes cooking is needed to brown outside and heat thoroughly. If parboiled rare, barbecue more slowly, until heated thoroughly.

BARBECUE SAUCE:
2/3 cup orange marmalade   Dash soy sauce
1/3 cup prepared barbecue
  sauce

The Sandlapper Cookbook

Jolie's Duck Au Vin

6 wild ducks
4 cups Burgundy
2 cloves garlic, minced
2 tablespoons fresh parsley,
  minced
1 bay leaf
2 teaspoons salt
1/2 teaspoon thyme
1/2 teaspoon pepper
1/4 cup soy sauce

1/4 cup salad oil
1/2 teaspoon ginger
1/4 teaspoon oregano
1/4 cup wine vinegar
4 chicken bouillon cubes
6 slices bacon
1 large onion, chopped
1 large bell pepper, sliced
1 pound mushrooms
Cornstarch

Place wild ducks in a large bowl. Mix next 13 ingredients well to be used as a marinade. Pour over ducks and refrigerate overnight. Place ducks, breast side down, in a covered roasting pan, and pour marinade over ducks. Bake at 275° for 3 hours. Sauté onion, bell pepper, and mushrooms in butter until just tender. Remove ducks from oven turning each one breast side up. Place the bacon on top of each duck, then add the onion/pepper/mushroom mixture. Cover, continue cooking for 1 hour. These are approximate cooking times, as ducks vary in size according to type. Ducks are done when meat pulls easily away from breast bone. Remove from oven, pour off broth, skimming off fat. Thicken broth with cornstarch and use as a gravy. Place ducks under broiler, if desired. Serve with wild rice.

Island Events Cookbook

More than two hundred private shooting preserves and some 1.2 million acres of public wildlife management lands provide a wealth of dove, quail, duck, squirrel, rabbit, fox, white-tailed deer, eastern wild turkey, and even wild hog hunting.

Roast Pheasant in Cranberry Sauce Flambé

Pheasants
1 small orange per bird
1/2 sliced apple per bird
2 onion slices per bird
Chopped celery
Salt and pepper
Melted butter

Cranberry sauce (whole
berry), about 1 can per bird
Angostura bitters
Juice of 1/2 lemon
Wine or pear vinegar
Cognac (about 1/2 cup per
2-3 pounds of bird)

Pluck but do not skin birds. Stuff cavity of birds starting with slices of orange, then add apple, onion and celery ending with end of orange to close the cavity. Cover and roast in a 350° oven for 1 hour. Uncover, remove some of the drippings and pour over hot cranberry sauce to which has been added a dash of angostura bitters, lemon juice and a dash of vinegar. Roast, uncovered, for at least 20 minutes more. Baste if necessary with pan juices. Place birds on hot platter or a chafing dish. Pour sauce over and flame with cognac. It's great!

The Museum Cookbook

Dove Bog

3 medium onions, chopped
4 stalks celery, chopped
1 teaspoon salt
2 teaspoons pepper

10 dove breasts
5 pieces raw chicken
1 1/2 pounds smoked sausage
2 cups raw rice

In 7-quart pot place onions, celery, salt, pepper, dove and chicken. Cover with water and boil covered about 45 minutes. Cut sausage into thick slices and add to pot. Continue cooking an additional 15 minutes. Remove dove, chicken and sausage; reserve broth. Debone chicken and dove. Cut into bite-size pieces. Measure broth, adding enough water, if necessary, to yield 4 cups. Return broth to pot, add rice and bring to boil. Cook on low 10 minutes. Add dove, chicken and sausage. Cook 10-15 minutes on medium, stirring occasionally. Can prepare ahead of time. Serves 8.

Uptown Down South

Carolina Quail

1 1/2 cups long-grain rice,
  uncooked
10 quail
1 can cream of mushroom soup

4 cups water
1 package dried onion soup
  mix

Place rice in bottom of shallow baking pan; add quail. Spoon mushroom soup over birds. Add water and sprinkle with onion soup mix. Cover pan with aluminum foil and bake 2 hours at 350°. Uncover last 10 minutes to brown. There is no need to add salt and pepper, as mushroom and onion soup mix contain adequate seasoning. Serves 5.

Southern Wildfowl and Wild Game Cookbook

Quail with Mushrooms and Onions

6 quail
Salt
Pepper
Paprika
6 slices bacon, boiled for 5
  minutes
1/2 cup lemon or lime juice

Sweet butter and olive oil
2 chopped onions
1 1/2 pounds fresh
  mushrooms
Some chopped pimentos
Wild rice, cooked

Pat quail dry with paper towels. Rub inside and out with mixture of salt, pepper and paprika. Fasten strip of bacon across breast of each quail.

Arrange birds in well-buttered baking pan and cover with lid or tin foil. Bake at around 350° or 400° for about an hour, basting every now and then with the citrus juice and pan drippings.

Meanwhile, melt a little butter with a little olive oil and sauté the onions, mushrooms and pimentos until just tender. Salt and pepper to taste.

Pour mushrooms and onions in platter. Put quail, when done, on top, and serve with wild rice.

Southeastern Wildlife Cookbook

Braised Rabbit

3 slices breakfast bacon,
  uncooked
1 ready-to-cook rabbit,
  quartered
1 small onion, chopped
1 clove garlic, peeled and
  chopped

1 teaspoon salt
1/2 teaspoon black pepper
1/2 teaspoon prepared herb
  seasoning
1 (16-ounce) can whole
  tomatoes

In large skillet on medium heat, cook bacon crisp. Remove and crumble. Sauté rabbit meat in drippings until brown on both sides. Add bacon and remaining ingredients. Cover; bring to boil. Reduce heat to simmer and cook 1 hour. Serves 4.

Southern Wildfowl and Wild Game Cookbook

Venison Meatloaf

1 package dry onion soup
1/2 cup hot water
2 pounds ground venison
1 egg
1 tablespoon Worcestershire
  sauce

1 teaspoon salt
1/2 teaspoon black pepper
1/2 cup bread crumbs

Pour onion soup into bowl, add hot water to dissolve. Combine with remaining ingredients, shape into loaf and bake at 350° 1 hour. Serves 8.

Southern Wildfowl and Wild Game Cookbook

Stir-Fried Venison
(A Wok Dish)

1/2 tablespoon vegetable oil
1 pound round or rump
roast (trim any gristle or
connective tissue and cut
into 1/4-inch slices across
the grain)
1 large clove garlic, minced
1 medium onion, thinly
sliced
1/2 - 1 cup bite-sized
broccoli
1 teaspoon fresh ginger,
minced
2 celery stalks, sliced

1/2 cup snow peas, trimmed
1/2 cup fresh mushrooms,
sliced
2 - 3 green onions cut into
1/2-inch sections
1 pound vegetables*
1/2 cup canned beef or
chicken stock
2 teaspoons salt (optional)
1 beaten egg
1/2 tablespoon sugar
1 tablespoon sherry
1 tablespoon cornstarch

Heat 1/2 tablespoon oil in a large wok, add half the meat slices and stir-fry until browned. Remove to the serving dish using a slotted spatula. Stir-fry the rest of the venison and remove to a dish. Add garlic and onion and stir-fry until tender. Add broccoli, ginger and celery and stir-fry one to two minutes. Add snow peas, mushrooms, green onions and other vegetables; stir-fry one minute, and add stock. Stir and simmer over medium heat until vegetables are almost done. Season. Mix remaining ingredients and pour over. Add venison to heat through and blend flavors.

Vegetables should be crisp and tender and venison should not be gray, but a little pink.

*Other additions or substitutions include sliced water chestnuts, bamboo shoots, cauliflower florets, carrots sliced into thin "coins" and green peppers.

Southeastern Wildlife Cookbook

Turkey Dressing

Cook giblets in saucepan
  and use broth for dressing
2 cups diced celery
3/4 cup minced onion
1/2 cup butter
4 cups dry bread crumbs

4 cups corn bread, crumbled
Salt and pepper to taste
1 tablespoon poultry
  seasoning (optional)
3 cups turkey broth
2 beaten eggs

Cook celery and onion for 5 minutes in butter. Add to bread crumbs and add seasoning. Mix remaining ingredients, except eggs, thoroughly; then add beaten eggs. Stir lightly. If dressing seems dry, add enough water to moisten well. Stuff turkey and bake remainder in baking dish, uncovered, for 45 minutes to an hour at 400°. Serve this in spoonfuls around turkey. Serves 12.

Nell Graydon's Cook Book

Pecan Turkey Stuffing

In 1672 Henry Hughes and some others surrendered land so that the town of Charleston might be built. Perhaps there is some esoteric connection between that and the fact that Mr. Edward Hughes has the most spacious garden and house in the city limits today. Distinguished guests go back to New York and Paris and London boasting to their friends about the pressed turkey and pecan of which they partook in Mr. Hughes' house. For this is more than a mere food; it is a confection. Mr. Hughes allowed us to copy the recipe from his mother's old notebook.

To the recipe was appended a note which read, "The most delicious stuffing that has ever been made. A choice old Charleston recipe." We see no reason to dispute this proclamation. This stuffing is especially good for boned turkey, and is, of course, only for the very greatest of state occasions.

CONTINUED

CONTINUED

1 turkey liver
12 slices toasted bread
1/4 cup butter
3 tablespoons lard
1 teaspoon salt
1 teaspoon black pepper
1 teaspoon celery seed,
  crushed
1 teaspoon dried Nabob
  thyme
1 tablespoon parsley,
  chopped fine

1/2 nutmeg, grated
6 hard-cooked eggs
1/4 teaspoon ground mace
2 cups salted pecans,
  chopped
1 can mushrooms, chopped
  fine
1/2 cup sherry
1 large onion
1 tablespoon lard

Boil the liver the day before the stuffing is made. Roll the toasted bread on a biscuit board, then sift through a colander into a large bowl and add the butter, lard, salt, black pepper, celery seed, thyme, parsley, and grated nutmeg. Pour in a little boiling water and mix thoroughly by hand. Add the whites of the hard-cooked eggs, riced, and the yolks rubbed smooth with the mace. Then add the salted pecans, mushrooms and sherry. Mix together thoroughly.

Put the onion, grated or finely minced, into a frying pan with the lard. When very hot, add the powdered liver and fry until brown. Allow to cool and then mix thoroughly with the other ingredients. Stuff the turkey, having first rubbed it with salt and black pepper both inside and outside.

Two Hundred Years of Charleston Cooking

Chestnut Stuffing

No game cook could ever feel competent without at least once concocting this stuffing. And this is the recipe that complements the wild turkey like none other.

2 cups chestnuts	**2 cups cracker crumbs**
1 tablespoon butter or margarine, melted	**1 cup milk**
	Salt and pepper to taste

Shell and skin 2 cups chestnuts; cover with water and boil until tender. Mash through colander. Add chestnuts to a mixture of the remaining ingredients. Makes about 4 cups.

Southern Wildfowl and Wild Game Cookbook

Sausage-Mushroom Stuffing

1/2 pound ground sausage	**4 cups cooked cornbread, crumbled**
1 tablespoon butter or margarine	**1/4 teaspoon thyme**
1 pound fresh mushrooms, sliced	**1/2 teaspoon marjoram**
1/2 cup onion, chopped	**2 cups chicken or turkey stock**
1/4 cup celery, chopped	**Salt and pepper to taste**

Cook sausage with butter in skillet until meat is brown and crumbly. Remove meat from pan. Add mushrooms, onion and celery and sauté 4-5 minutes. Return meat to pan, add cornbread and seasonings and mix. Remove to large bowl and add chicken stock to moisten. Makes 6-7 cups. Excellent with turkey, goose, duck, pheasant, grouse and small game birds.

Southern Wildfowl and Wild Game Cookbook

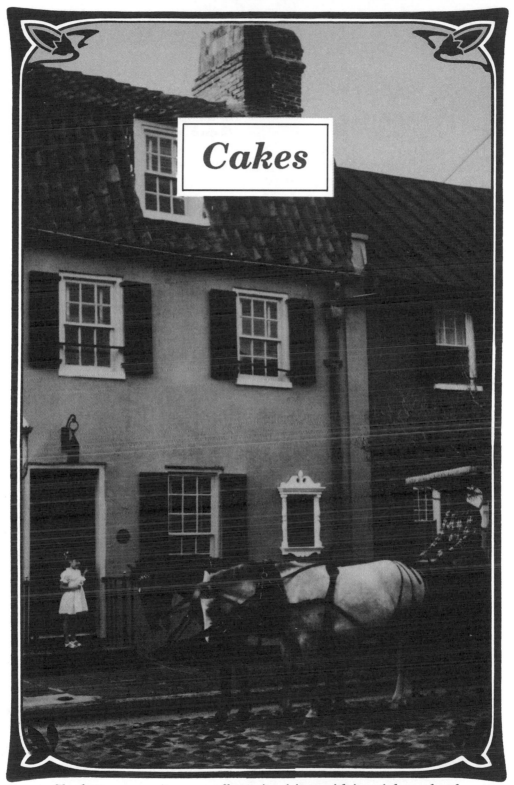

Cakes

Charleston weaves its own spell over its visitors with its rainbow colored houses, carriage rides, fine antique stores and elegant dining spots.

Miss Lucy's Coconut Cake

1 cup butter	1/2 teaspoon salt
2 cups sugar	1/2 cup buttermilk
4 eggs	1/2 cup water
3 cups all-purpose flour	1 teaspoon vanilla
3 teaspoons baking powder (scant)	

Cream butter and sugar. Add eggs, one at a time, beating well after each addition. Sift together dry ingredients and add alternately with buttermilk and water, which have been mixed. Add vanilla and blend thoroughly. Turn into 3 greased, paper lined cake pans. Bake in a 375° oven for about 20 minutes. Remove from oven; let stand in pans a few minutes, then turn out on rack to cool slightly before putting together with the filling.

FILLING FOR COCONUT CAKE:

Large fresh coconut, grated (reserve milk from coconut)	1 cup coconut milk (supplement with sweet milk, if necessary, to make 1 cup)
2 cups sugar	
2 tablespoons cornstarch	

Reserve 3/4-cup grated coconut, then mix remaining coconut with other ingredients. Place over medium heat and cook, stirring until thickened. Cool slightly. Spread between layers, sprinkling a bit of grated coconut on top of filling on each layer. Spread over top and sides of cake. Sprinkle grated coconut on top of cake.

Seasoned with Light

 Gullah is a curious-sounding language spoken by some of the Lowcountry black people. It's a combination of King's English, American English and an African dialect.

Mama's Crunch Pound Cake

1 cup shortening
2 cups sugar
6 eggs
2 cups all-purpose flour
1 1/2 teaspoons lemon
  flavoring

2/3 teaspoon vanilla
3/4 teaspoon salt
2 tablespoons sour cream

Cream shortening and sugar at medium speed. Add eggs one at a time, beating well. Add flour in three parts; mix well. Add flavorings, salt and sour cream. Pour into a greased and floured Bundt or tube pan. Place into a cold oven. Set oven temperature for 300° and bake for 1 hour. Test for doneness with a toothpick.

Note: Cake has a crunchy top.

Thoroughbred Fare

Bill Brown's Pound Cake

1 pound margarine
3 cups sugar
1 tablespoon shortening
  (rounded)
10 large eggs

2 teaspoons vanilla
1 teaspoon almond
2 teaspoons lemon
1/4 teaspoon ground mace
4 cups flour

Cream margarine, sugar and shortening. Add whole eggs, one at a time, beating after each addition. Add flavoring, then flour. Turn into greased tube pan. Place in cold oven. Bake at 300° for 1 1/2 hours.

GLAZE:

2 cups powdered sugar
1 lemon rind, grated

3 tablespoons lemon juice
1/2 tablespoon water

Mix ingredients together (add more water if needed, but be sure not to get too thin). Spoon on top of cake and let run down sides.

Seasoned with Light

Fulton Plantation Apricot Pound Cake

CAKE:

2 sticks unsalted butter, softened

3 cups sugar

6 large eggs

1 cup sour cream

2/3 cup apricot brandy

1 teaspoon vanilla

1 teaspoon orange extract

1 1/2 teaspoons rum

3 cups sifted all-purpose flour

1/2 teaspoon salt

1/4 teaspoon baking soda

Preheat oven to 325°. In a large bowl, cream the butter, adding sugar a little at a time. Beat until light and fluffy. Add eggs while beating, one at a time. Add sour cream, brandy, vanilla, orange extract, and rum. Sift together flour, salt, and baking soda in separate bowl. Add dry ingredients to butter mixture and stir. Transfer batter to well-buttered and floured 2 1/2-quart Bundt pan. Bake one hour or until cake tester inserted in center comes out clean. Let cook in pan on rack for one hour.

TOPPING:

2 dozen Turkish apricots

1/2 cup apricot brandy

1/4 cup rum

1/2 cup unsalted butter

1 tablespoon cornstarch

1/2 cup light brown sugar

2 teaspoons milk

Mince 16 apricots in food processor with metal blade. Soak these apricots in the brandy and rum for at least 4 hours. After marinating, combine all ingredients in small saucepan over low heat and stir constantly until thickened. Spoon slightly cooled mixture over cake and decorate with remaining 8 apricots. Yields 1 (2 1/2-quart) Bundt cake.

Charleston Receipts Repeats

Apricot Almond Cake

1 cup butter, soft
2 cups sugar
2 eggs
1 cup sour cream
1 teaspoon almond extract
2 cups flour

1 teaspoon baking powder
1 teaspoon salt
1 cup slivered almonds
1 (10-ounce) jar apricot
    preserves

Preheat oven to 350°. Cream butter and sugar until light. Beat in the eggs, one at a time. Fold in sour cream and extract. Sift flour, baking powder and salt and fold in. Put a third of the mixture in a greased and floured tube pan. Spread half of the almonds and half of the apricot preserves over the batter. Spoon in rest of the batter. Add remaining preserves and top with remaining almonds. Bake for 1 hour and 10 minutes at 350°. Yield: 16 servings.

Per Serving: Calories 379; Protein 4 g; Cholesterol 71 mg; Fiber 1 g
Percent of Calories: Protein 4%; Carbohydrates 52%; Fat 44%

Palmetto Evenings

Pineapple Upside Down Cake

1/3 cup butter
1/2 cup chopped nuts
1 cup light brown sugar
1 large can sliced pineapple
1/2 cup butter
1 cup sugar

2 eggs
1 1/2 cups flour
1/2 cup milk
1/2 teaspoon vanilla
1 teaspoon baking powder

Melt 1/3 cup butter in iron skillet (or 9x13-inch pan). Mix nuts with brown sugar and spread over butter. Lay pineapple slices evenly over mixture. Cream 1/2 cup butter and 1 cup sugar. Add eggs, beating well after each. Add flour and milk, a little at a time. Then add vanilla and baking powder. Pour over pineapple and bake at 350° for 30 minutes. Let stand about 5 minutes; then invert. Serves 10-12.

Nell Graydons' Cook Book

Bluffton's Praline Cake

1 cup buttermilk
1/2 cup butter or oleo
2 eggs
2 cups brown sugar
2 tablespoons vanilla

2 cups plain flour
2 tablespoons cocoa
 (heaping)
12 teaspoon soda

Place buttermilk and butter or oleo in saucepan and warm. Put into a bowl and add eggs, brown sugar and vanilla. Beat a minute or two. Sift together all dry ingredients. Add to wet mixture. Beat well. Pour into greased and floured 9x13-inch pan and bake for 20-25 minutes at 350°. Spread top of cake with the following icing as soon as cake is done.

ICING:
1 cup brown sugar
1 stick butter or oleo,
 softened

6 tablespoons cream or
 top milk
1 cup pecans, chopped

Mix all ingredients together and spread on cake. Place cake in oven and turn on broil until bubbles form on icing and it turns a light brown. It is better to put in lower part of oven for this. Serves 10-12 generously.

Bluffton's Favorite Recipes

Poppy Seed Cake

1/2 pound butter
1 1/2 cups sugar
4 eggs, separated
1 (2-ounce) package poppy
  seeds

1 teaspoon baking soda
1 cup sour cream
2 cups cake flour or 1 3/4
  cups plain flour
1 teaspoon vanilla

Cream butter and sugar until light. Beat egg yolks and mix with poppy seeds. Add to butter mixture. Add soda and sour cream, then flour and vanilla. Fold in stiffly beaten egg whites. Bake in a 10-inch ungreased tube pan at 350° for 1 hour.

Flavored With Tradition

Black Russian Cake

1 (18.5-ounce) package
  yellow cake mix
1 (3-ounce) package instant
  chocolate pudding
4 eggs
1 cup vegetable oil
1/2 cup chopped pecans

3/4 cup water
1/2 cup Kahlua liqueur
1/4 cup vodka
1 cup powdered sugar
  (optional)
2 tablespoons Kahlua
  (optional)

Combine first 8 ingredients and mix well. Pour into a greased and floured 10-inch tube pan. Bake in a 350° oven for 55-60 minutes. Glaze, if desired, with 1 cup powdered sugar and enough Kahlua to drizzle.

The Sandlappers' Salvation Cookbook

Strawberry Cake

1 box yellow cake mix
4 eggs
1 cup cooking oil
1/2 cup boiling water

1 regular box strawberry
  gelatin
5-ounces frozen strawberries

Combine cake mix, eggs, one at a time, and oil. Add strawberry gelatin with 1/2 cup boiling water. Mix well and add the strawberries. Cook in a stem pan 325°, 1 hour.

Carolina Cuisine

Brownstone Cake

1 cup butter (2 sticks)	2 squares chocolate, melted
2 cups sugar	1 cup buttermilk
3 unbeaten eggs	1 cup hot water
3 cups flour (do not sift before measuring)	2 teaspoons baking soda
	1 teaspoon vanilla

Cream butter and sugar. Add eggs, one at a time. Add melted chocolate and flour, a small amount at a time, with the buttermilk. Dissolve soda in very hot water and add last with the vanilla. Pour in pans and bake at 375° for about 20-25 minutes. Makes 3 layers.

FILLING:

1 box light brown sugar	1 teaspoon vanilla
1/2 cup butter (1 stick)	1 cup chopped nuts
3/4 cup Carnation milk (1 small can)	

Put first three ingredients together in a heavy saucepan. Bring to a boil and cook 3 minutes, stirring constantly. Remove from heat and set saucepan in cold water. Continue beating until right consistency is reached for spreading. Add 1 teaspoon vanilla, 1 cup chopped pecans or walnuts (I like walnuts better). Put filling between layers and top of cake.

Olivia's Favorite Menus and Recipes

Plum Nutty Cake

1 cup Wesson or Mazola oil	1 teaspoon ground cinnamon
2 cups white sugar	1 teaspoon lemon extract
2 1/2 cups self-rising flour	2 small jars plum or prune baby food
3 eggs	
1 teaspoon ground cloves	1 cup finely chopped nuts

Combine Wesson oil and sugar. Then mix in flour, eggs, ground cloves, ground cinnamon, lemon extract and plum or prune baby food. After this is mixed well, add nuts. Grease Bundt pan. Bake at 325° for 55 minutes. (Start in cold oven.)

Feeding the Faithful

Butter Pecan Cake

1 1/3 cups chopped pecans	2 cups sugar
1 1/4 cups butter	4 unbeaten eggs
3 cups sifted plain flour	1 cup milk
2 teaspoons baking powder	2 tablespoons vanilla
1/2 teaspoon salt	

Toast pecans in 1/4 cup butter in a 350° oven for 20-25 minutes. Stir frequently. Sift flour with baking powder and salt. Cream 1 cup butter; gradually add sugar, creaming well. Blend in eggs; beat well after each. Add dry ingredients alternately with milk, beginning and ending with dry ingredients. Blend well after each addition. Stir in vanilla and 1 1/3 cups pecans. Turn into three 8 or 9-inch round layer cake pans, greased and floured on bottoms. Bake at 350° for 25-30 minutes. Cool 15 minutes. Remove from pans. Wait until completely cooled before frosting between layers and on top.

BUTTER PECAN FROSTING:

1/4 cup butter	4-6 tablespoons evaporated
1 pound sifted	milk
confectioners' sugar	2/3 cup pecans
1 teaspoon vanilla	

Cream butter. Add 1 pound (4-4 1/2 cups) sifted confectioners' sugar, vanilla and evaporated milk or heavy cream until of spreading consistency. Stir in pecans.

The Sandlappers' Salvation Cookbook

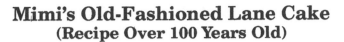

Mimi's Old-Fashioned Lane Cake
(Recipe Over 100 Years Old)

1 (12-ounce) box raisins, cut up
1 small package dates, cut up
1 (9-ounce) package frozen coconut, thawed
1 quart chopped nuts
Grated rind of 1 lemon
1/2 cup bourbon
1 1/2 cups butter or margarine
2 cups sugar
6 egg whites
3 cups plain flour
1 teaspoon soda
1 cup buttermilk

Before making cake, soak the first five ingredients in the bourbon. Preheat oven to 350°. Grease and flour 4 (9-inch) cake pans. Cream butter and sugar. Add one egg white at a time and two tablespoons of flour alternately. Dissolve soda in 1/4 cup of the buttermilk and add with the rest of the buttermilk. Bake until straw comes out clean. Allow to cool.

FILLING:
6 egg yolks
3 whole eggs
2 cups sugar
1 stick butter or oleo

Combine egg yolks, whole eggs, sugar and butter in double boiler and cook until thick enough to spread. Add ingredients which have been soaking in bourbon. Cook a little longer and spread between cake layers when all cool. Any leftover filling may be frozen and used at another time. Ice top and sides with any good recipe for white icing.

Note: Frozen coconut was not available 100 years ago, but it saves time and is just as good!

The Museum Cookbook

 You'll find sweetgrass baskets in the Lowcountry (land along the coast) and pinestraw baskets in the Upstate.

Lady Baltimore Cake I

Each year at Christmas time hundreds of white boxes go out of Charleston to all parts of the country bearing the round, the tall, the light, the fragile, the ineffable Lady Baltimore cakes. There are several ladies of old descent who make an excellent living baking these famous cakes. You have seen Lady Baltimore cakes on many a menu, but it usually means something altogether different from the real Charleston delicacy.

By no stretch of the imagination could this cake be called economical, but its goodness makes one willing to forget its eight eggs! Half of the cake, however, will make three medium-sized layers.

1 cup butter	4 teaspoons baking powder
2 cups sugar	1 cup milk
8 eggs, separated	1 teaspoon almond extract
4 cups flour	

Cream the butter and sugar, add the beaten egg yolks and beat well. Mix and sift the dry ingredients and add alternately with the milk to the first mixture. Flavor with almond extract and last of all add the stiffly beaten egg whites. Turn into well-greased layer cake pans and bake in a moderately hot oven (375°) for about twenty-five minutes.

THE LEMON FILLING REQUIRES:

3 cups sugar	1 teaspoon vanilla
1/2 cup lemon juice	2 cups chopped walnuts
1/4 cup boiling water	2 cups seeded raisins
4 egg whites	

Add the lemon juice and water to the sugar and cook until it spins a long thread, or to 246°. Pour the hot syrup over the stiffly beaten egg whites, beating constantly, and continue beating until cold and stiff enough to hold its shape. Flavor with vanilla and add the chopped nuts and raisins. Spread between layers of cake and on top and sides.

Two Hundred Years of Charleston Cooking

Huguenot Torte

4 eggs
3 cups sugar
8 tablespoons flour
5 teaspoons baking powder
1/2 teaspoon salt

2 cups chopped tart cooking
  apples
2 cups chopped pecans or
  walnuts
2 teaspoons vanilla

Beat whole eggs in electric mixer or with rotary beater until very frothy and lemon-colored. Add other ingredients in above order. Pour into two well-buttered baking pans about 8x12 inches. Bake in 325° oven about 45 minutes or until crusty and brown. To serve, scoop up with pancake turner (keeping crusty part on top), pile on large plate and cover with whipped cream and a sprinkling of the chopped nuts, or make 16 individual servings.

Charleston Receipts

Lemon Pecan Fruit Cake

1 pound butter
1 pound light brown sugar
6 eggs, separated
4 cups flour (plain)
1 teaspoon baking powder
1/2 teaspoon salt

1 1/2 ounces pure lemon
  extract
1 pound pecans
1/2 pound candied cherries
1/2 pound candied pineapple

Cream butter and sugar well, add egg yolks one at a time, beating well after each. Sift 2 cups of flour with baking powder and salt. Add lemon extract alternately with flour to cream mixture. Dredge nuts and fruit with remaining flour and add to mixture. Fold in stiffly beaten egg whites. Put batter in well greased tube pan or 3 small loaf pans. Let stand overnight. Bake at 225° for 2 hours and 45 minutes. When removing from pan, turn cake upside down and leave upside down so butter will drain through cake. This cake is always a favorite during the holidays—a Tallon family favorite.

One Course At A Time

Pinto Fiesta Cake

1 cup sugar
1/4 cup butter
2 eggs
2 cups cooked pinto beans, mashed
1 cup all-purpose flour
1 teaspoon baking soda
1/2 teaspoon salt

1 teaspoon cinnamon
1/2 teaspoon cloves
1/2 teaspoon allspice
1 cup raisins
1 teaspoon vanilla
2 cups raw apples, peeled and diced
1/2 cup chopped nuts

Cream sugar and butter. Add beaten eggs and mashed beans. Combine flour, baking soda, salt, cinnamon, cloves and allspice. Add dry ingredients to creamed mixture. Mix raisins, vanilla, apples and nuts. Add to cake mixture. Pour into a deep, well-greased 9-inch layer pan. Bake at 375° for 45 minutes.

ICING:

1/2 cup margarine or butter
1 (8-ounce) package cream cheese

1 box powdered sugar
3/4 cup chopped pecans
2 teaspoons vanilla

Melt butter. Add other ingredients. Spread over cake when cooled. Store cake in refrigerator.

Thoroughbred Fare

Chocolate Roll

6 eggs, separated
1 cup sugar
1/2 cup all-purpose flour
1/2 cup cocoa
1 teaspoon baking powder
2 cups whipping cream

Beat egg yolks and sugar until thick and lemon colored. Add flour, cocoa and baking powder. When blended, fold in beaten egg whites. Put mixture in a 17 1/2 x 12 1/2 x 1 1/2-inch greased pan lined with greased waxed paper. Bake at 400° for 12-15 minutes. Turn out onto towel or smooth surface. Remove waxed paper and roll tightly. When cold, unroll and spread with whipped cream. Roll up and spread top with icing.

ICING:
2 1/2 squares bitter
  chocolate
1/2 stick butter
2 cups powdered sugar
1/4 teaspoon salt
1 teaspoon vanilla
2 tablespoons evaporated
  milk

Melt chocolate and butter. Add powdered sugar, salt, and vanilla. Put in electric mixer and add canned milk for proper consistency to spread.

"Don't Forget the Parsley...."

Orange Cranberry Torte

2 1/4 cups sifted
  all-purpose flour
1 cup sugar
1/4 teaspoon salt
1 teaspoon baking powder
1 teaspoon baking soda
1 cup chopped English
  walnuts

1 cup diced dates
1 cup fresh cranberries
Grated rind of 2 oranges
2 eggs, beaten
1 cup buttermilk
3/4 cup salad oil
1 cup orange juice
1 1/2 cups brown sugar

Heat oven to 350°. Sift together into bowl flour, sugar, salt, baking powder, soda. Stir in nuts, dates, cranberries, orange rind. Combine eggs, buttermilk and salad oil. Add to flour and fruit mixture. Pour into well greased 10-inch tube pan. Bake 1 hour. Let stand in pan until lukewarm. Remove to rack placed over wide dish. Combine orange juice and brown sugar. Heat until dissolved. Pour over cake. Pour drippings over cake again. Wrap in foil. Tastes good warm or a couple of days old.

Culinary Crinkles

Almond Crusted Torte

1 2/3 cups plain flour
1 1/2 cups sugar
1 cup butter, melted
1/8 teaspoon salt

2 tablespoons almond extract
2 eggs, beaten
No-stick vegetable spray
2 1/4 ounces sliced almonds

Stir together all ingredients except almonds. Pour into 10-inch pie pan that has been sprayed with no-stick vegetable product. Sprinkle almonds over top. Bake at 350° for 35-40 minutes or until lightly browned. Serves 8.

Uptown Down South

Brandy Pudding Cake

1 (1-ounce) square
  unsweetened chocolate
1/2 cup softened butter
1 cup sugar

2 eggs
1/2 cup unsifted flour
1/4 cup cognac
Vanilla ice cream

Heat oven 350°. Lightly butter 9-inch square cake pan. Place chocolate in top of double boiler and heat over hot, not boiling water, stirring occasionally. Beat in butter, sugar and eggs until well blended and smooth. Gradually add flour and beat just enough to combine. Stir in cognac. Pour batter into prepared pan. Bake 25 minutes. Do not over bake. Serve warm with ice cream.

Culinary Crinkles

Sunken Treasure Cake

1 package Pillsbury Plus
  German chocolate cake mix
1 cup water

1/3 cup oil
3 eggs
1 bag crushed Heath bars

Preheat oven to 350°. Grease 13x9-inch pan. In large bowl, combine all cake ingredients, except candy bars, at low speed until moistened; beat 2 minutes at highest speed. Pour into prepared pan. Sprinkle batter with crushed Heath bars. Bake at 350° for 30-40 minutes. Cool completely.

GLAZE:
1 cup powdered sugar
5 teaspoons water

1 teaspoon vanilla

In small bowl, blend glaze ingredients. Drizzle over cooled cake.

Seasoned with Light

Chocolate Grand Marnier Gateau

CHOCOLATE CAKE:

6 ounces semi-sweet
  chocolate
1/2 cup granulated sugar
1/4 cup water

6 egg yolks
6 egg whites, stiffly beaten
1 tablespoon strong coffee

Preheat oven to 375°. Melt chocolate in double boiler. Mix sugar and water in a saucepan and bring to a boil. Cook for 2 minutes over medium heat. Place egg yolks in above. Slowly pour hot sugar syrup over yolks, beating vigorously with whisk for 5 minutes, until it is light, smooth, and pale in color. Mix in chocolate and coffee. Add a third of the egg whites to chocolate mixture and mix with a whisk. Add remaining whites and fold with a spatula—just enough to combine. Do not overwork. Spread on a sheet pan lined with buttered wax paper, about 1/2-inch thick. Bake cake in 375° oven for 15 minutes until cake is springy to touch. Cool at room temperature. Cover with plastic wrap and cool for 2 hours.

CHOCOLATE FILLING:

11 ounces semi-sweet
  chocolate
4 ounces unsweetened
  chocolate
Pinch cream of tartar

2 egg whites, room
  temperature
3 tablespoons grand marnier
  liqueur
3 1/2 cups heavy cream

Melt chocolate over simmering water. Let rest on table for 10 minutes. Beat egg whites with cream of tartar. Fold into chocolate and add grand marnier. Whip cream until stiff and fold into above mixture. Chill in refrigerator for at least 1/2 hour. Line a loaf pan with wax paper bottom and sides. Cover with chocolate cake, cut a long piece first to fit the bottom of the loaf pan. Cut pieces to stand up in the sides. Fill with chocolate filling to the top edge of the cake. Cover the entire length with the remaining cake. Chill for two hours. Remove from pan, discard wax paper and slice into about 1-inch pieces. Serve with a plain vanilla sauce. Serves 12. From Robert's of Charleston.

Charleston Receipts Repeats

Angel Food Charlotte Russe Cake

1 cup sifted cake flour	1 1/4 teaspoons cream
1 1/2 cups sugar	of tartar
1 1/4 cups egg whites	1 teaspoon vanilla extract
1/4 teaspoon salt	1/4 teaspoon almond extract

Sift flour before measuring, then sift four times with 1/2 cup of the sugar. Sift remaining cup of sugar. Add salt to egg whites and beat until foamy. Add cream of tartar; beat until they hold in peaks. Add sifted sugar a few tablespoons at a time, beating after each addition. Fold in vanilla and almond extracts. Fold in flour and sugar mixture 1/2 cup at a time. Pour into angel food cake pan and bake in moderate oven of 375° for 35 minutes. Turn pan upside down and let cake cool for an hour before removing.

FILLING:

1/4 cup cool water	1 cup whipping cream
1 envelope gelatin	1/2 cup sugar
3/4 cup sherry	

Dissolve gelatin in water. Heat sherry to boiling point; stir into gelatin mixture. Let cool. Whip cream, add sugar and fold into cooled gelatin mixture. Let congeal in refrigerator. Cut cake into two layers and place filling between layers and in hole. Ice with the following icing:

ICING:

4 egg whites	1/8 teaspoon cream of tartar
1 cup sugar	
1 tablespoon corn syrup	
(white)	

Place all ingredients in top of double-boiler and heat, stirring occasionally, until very hot. Pour into small bowl of electric mixer and beat at high speed ten minutes or until it holds in peaks. Let cake stand overnight in refrigerator before serving. Serves 8-10. This cake can be frozen very successfully if wrapped in heavy paper. Remove paper before starting to thaw cake to keep icing intact.

Charleston Receipts

Amaretto Cheese Cake

We have sold the book for this recipe alone!

CRUST:

1 1/2 cups graham cracker crumbs

2 tablespoons sugar

1 teaspoon cinnamon

1 stick plus 2 tablespoons butter, melted

FILLING:

3 (8-ounce) packages cream cheese, softened

1 cup sugar

4 eggs

1/3 cup amaretto

TOPPING:

1 cup sour cream

1 tablespoons amaretto

2 tablespoons sugar

GARNISH:

1/2 cup roasted almonds, optional

1 tablespoon grated chocolate, optional

Mix all the ingredients together for the crust and press into bottom of 8 or 9-inch springform pan and up the sides 1/2 inch. For the filling, beat the cream cheese until it is fluffy. Gradually add 1 cup sugar. Add eggs one at at time beating well after each. Stir in 1/3 cup amaretto and pour into pan. Bake at 375° for 45-50 minutes. Remove from oven and turn oven to 500°. For the topping, mix the topping ingredients and pour over the cheese cake and put in the oven for 5 minutes at 500°. Let the cake cool to room temperature and then refrigerate for 24-48 hours to ripen. Decorate with roasted almonds and grated chocolate. Yield: 16 slices. Make a day or two ahead.

Calories 420.75, Protein 49.97gm, Fat 30.80gm, Carbohydrates 29.81gm, Fiber 0.17gm, Cholesterol 150.70mg, Saturated Fats 15.63gm, Iron 0.79mg, Calcium 66.52mg, Sodium 289.85mg, Potassium 149.47mg, Vitamin A 1236.86 I.U., Vitamin C 0.14mg, Thiamine 0.06mg, Riboflavin 0.23mg, Niacin 0.39mg

The Enlightened Gourmet

Amaretto Cake

1 ready-to-eat Angel Food
   cake (loaf or tube type)
Amaretto

1/2 gallon ice cream (any
   flavor)
1 large carton Cool Whip

Split cake into 3 sections horizontally. Place first section on cake plate. Drizzle 3 tablespoons amaretto over cake. Cover with 2 inches of ice cream.

Place second section of cake on top of ice cream layer. Drizzle with 3 tablespoons of amaretto. Cover with 2 inches of ice cream. Place third section of cake on top of ice cream. Drizzle with 3 tablespoons of amaretto. Fold 3 tablespoons of amaretto into large carton of Cool Whip. Ice cake. Freeze.

Note: Amaretto keeps cake from freezing hard, so you can remove it from freezer and serve immediately.

Cooking on the Go

Cookies and Candies

"A kiss for good luck?" These beautiful Aiken thoroughbreds are neighbors
at Dogwood Stables.

Pecan Crispies

1/2 cup shortening
1/2 cup butter
1 cup sugar
1 1/2 cups brown sugar
2 beaten eggs

2 1/2 cups flour
1/4 teaspoon salt
1/2 teaspoon soda
1 cup chopped nuts

Cream shortening, butter and sugars, add eggs and beat well. Add sifted dry ingredients and nut meats. Drop from teaspoon about 2 inches apart onto greased baking sheet. Bake in moderate oven 350° 12 to 15 minutes. Makes 5 dozen cookies.

The South Carolina Cook Book

Pecan Drops

1/2 cup butter
1/2 cup plus 2 tablespoons
  shortening
1 cup powdered sugar

2 1/2 cups cake flour
1 cup nuts, coarsely chopped
2 teaspoons vanilla

Cream butter and shortening. Add sugar. Gradually add flour, then nuts and vanilla. Drop on an ungreased cookie sheet. Bake at 325° for 10-12 minutes. (They do not turn brown.) Yield: 4 1/2 dozen.

Thoroughbred Fare

Very Thin Benne Cookies

3/4 cup melted butter (1 1/2
  sticks)
1 1/2 cups dark brown sugar
1 egg
3/4 cup flour

1/4 teaspoon baking powder
1/4 teaspoon salt
1 cup benne seed
1 teaspoon vanilla

Cream butter and sugar. Add egg slightly beaten; add flour with baking powder, salt, and benne seed. Add vanilla. Drop with a coffee spoon in pan lined with aluminum foil. Bake in 300° oven till brown. Let cool before removing from pan.

Charleston Receipts

Pat's Melt-Away Sugar Cookies

These get raves from everyone and make dozens!

1 cup butter, softened	2 eggs
1 cup vegetable oil	4 1/2 cups sifted flour
1 cup sugar	1 teaspoon baking soda
1 cup powdered sugar, unsifted	1 teaspoon salt
1 teaspoon vanilla extract	1 teaspoon cream of tartar

Mix together the butter, oil and sugars. Add vanilla and eggs. Sift together flour, soda, salt and cream of tartar and add to above mixture. Mix well. Chill overnight. Roll into balls about teaspoon size. Place on ungreased cookie sheets. Flatten with a fork. Bake at 300° for 12-15 minutes. Yield: 8-10 dozen.

Prescriptions for Good Eating

Kool-Aid Sugar Cookies

3/4 cup shortening	3 cups plain flour
1 stick margarine	3/4 teaspoon salt
2/3 cup sugar	2 1/2 teaspoons baking powder
1 cup presweetened Kool-Aid	
2 eggs	

Cream shortening, margarine, sugar and Kool-Aid. Add eggs. Mix remaining ingredients together and add to sugar mixture. Mix well. Refrigerate overnight. Roll dough 1/4-inch thick. Cut with cookie cutters. Bake at 375° for 7-10 minutes on an ungreased cookie sheet. May use any flavor Kool-Aid. Cherry is delicious and pretty for Christmas or Valentine's Day.

Carolina Cuisine Encore!

Butter Cookies

1 3/4 cups all-purpose flour
1/2 teaspoon baking powder
2/3 cup soft butter
1/2 cup sugar
1 small egg, well beaten

1/2 teaspoon vanilla
 flavoring
3/4 square chocolate, if
 desired

Sift flour, measure and resift with baking powder. Cream butter thoroughly; add sugar and continue creaming until well mixed. Stir in the well beaten egg. Add vanilla. Mix in sifted dry ingredients in 2 or 3 portions until dough is just smooth. If some chocolate cookies are desired, add chocolate, (which has been melted and cooled) to half the dough. Roll out 1/8-inch thick on a floured board and cut into desired shapes.

A finish or topping may be used on cookies before baking by using 1 beaten egg white and 1 teaspoon water and brush the tops of cookies with this mixture, sprinkle with sugar, chopped nuts, blanched almonds, candied fruit, chocolate sprinkles, etc. Bake on ungreased cookie sheet in a 400° oven for 6-8 minutes or until delicately browned. Cool on cake racks. Makes 3-4 dozen cookies.

Note: 1/2 teaspoon lemon extract and 1/4 teaspoon mace may be used in place of vanilla flavoring.

Stirrin' The Pots On Daufuskie

Lemon Love Notes

1/2 cup butter
1 cup sifted flour
1/4 cup confectioners' sugar
1 cup sugar
2 tablespoons flour

1/2 teaspoon baking powder
2 eggs, beaten
2 tablespoons lemon juice
2 teaspoons grated lemon
  rind

Mix butter, 1 cup flour and confectioners' sugar. Press in ungreased 8-inch square pan. Bake in 350° oven 8 minutes or until golden. Cool in pan on rack.

Combine sugar, 2 tablespoons flour and baking powder. Add eggs, lemon juice and peel. Mix well. Pour evenly over baked, cooled mixture in pan. Bake in 350° oven 25 minutes (top puffs up in baking and falls in cooling). Cool in pan on rack. Cut 2-inch squares. Sprinkle with confectioners' sugar.

Bethel Food Bazaar II

Peach Cookies

1/2 cup margarine or butter
1 cup sugar
1 large egg
2 cups all-purpose flour
1/2 teaspoon baking soda
1/4 teaspoon each, nutmeg
  and cinnamon

1/8 teaspoon each, ginger,
  ground cloves, salt
3 medium fresh ripe
  peaches
1/2 cup raisins, if desired

Cream margarine or butter and sugar in a bowl. Add egg and beat until light and fluffy. In another bowl, mix flour, baking soda and seasonings. Stir flour mixture into egg mixture, a little at a time. Peel, pit and finely dice peaches; stir into cookie mixture. Stir in raisins, if desired. Drop dough by rounded teaspoonsful onto cookie sheet. Bake at 375° for 20 minutes until cookies are browned on top. Cool thoroughly on wire rack before storing. Yield: about 4 dozen 2 1/2-inch cookies.

Note: These are soft, cake-like cookies. If cookies become too soft on standing, put them into a warm 250-300° oven for a few minutes.

The Peach Sampler

Oatmeal Lace Cookies

Nice for an afternoon tea.

2 cups quick oats	1/2 teaspoon salt
2 cups sugar	1 teaspoon vanilla
1 cup butter, melted	2 eggs
6 tablespoons flour	1/2 teaspoon baking powder

Preheat oven to 350°. Mix ingredients in order listed. Line cookie sheets with tin foil. Drop 1/2 teaspoon batter on cookie sheet, spacing two inches between. Bake 8-10 minutes. Cool on foil on cake racks. Peel from foil when cooled. Yields 200 cookies.

Charleston Receipts Repeats

Chewy Oatmeal Cookies

1 1/2 cups Crisco	2 teaspoon cinnamon
2 2/3 cups brown sugar	1/2 teaspoon nutmeg
4 eggs	2 1/4 cups flour
2 teaspoons vanilla	4 cups uncooked oatmeal
1 1/2 teaspoon soda	2 cups raisins (optional)
1 teaspoon salt	

Combine Crisco, brown sugar, eggs, and vanilla. Add soda, salt, cinnamon, nutmeg, and flour. Mix well. Stir in oatmeal and raisins. Drop by teaspoonfuls onto greased cookie sheet and bake for 8-10 minutes at 350°.

FILLING:

6 tablespoons flour	1/4 teaspoon salt
1 cup milk	1 teaspoon vanilla
1 cup Crisco	2 cups powdered sugar

Boil flour and milk until thick. Cool until cold. Then add Crisco, salt, vanilla, and powdered sugar. Beat. Put filling between 2 cookies.

500 Favorite Recipes

Filbert Christmas Cookies

1 pound filberts (in shells)
3/4 pound red and green
  candied cherries
1/2 pound whole dates
1/2 pound seeded prunes
1/2 cup soft butter
1 1/2 cup packed light brown
  sugar
2 eggs

1 teaspoon vanilla
2 1/2 cups sifted flour
1 teaspoon baking powder
1 teaspoon soda
1/2 teaspoon salt
1/2 teaspoon cinnamon
1/4 teaspoon nutmeg
1 cup sour cream

Shell nuts. Toast shelled nuts at 325° for 10 minutes. Stuff fruit with 1 whole nut each. Cream butter and sugar until fluffy. Beat in eggs and vanilla. Add sifted dry ingredients and spices alternately with sour cream. Carefully stir in stuffed fruit. Drop from spoon onto greased cookie sheet. Bake at 400 for 8-10 minutes; cool. Top with Brown Butter Frosting if desired. Makes 10-12 dozen.

BROWN BUTTER FROSTING:
3/4 cup butter
4 1/2 cups sifted
  confectioners' sugar

1/3 cup water

Lightly brown butter. Remove from heat; add confectioners' sugar and vanilla. Add water and beat.

These are soft, moist cookies. Do not stack unless you put waxed paper between layers. One of the most delicious cookies I have ever eaten; European in flavor.

The Sandlappers' Salvation Cookbook

Tea Time Tassies

CRUST:

1 (3-ounce) package cream cheese	**1/2 cup margarine**
	1 cup sifted flour (plain)

Let cheese and margarine soften; blend. Stir in flour. Chill about one hour; shape into 24 one-inch balls. Place in ungreased muffin pan. Press dough into bottom and sides, forming a pastry cup.

FILLING:

1 egg	**Dash of salt**
3/4 - 1 cup brown sugar	**2/3 - 3/4 cup pecans,**
1 tablespoon soft margarine	**chopped**
1 teaspoon vanilla extract	

Beat egg with sugar, margarine, vanilla, and salt until smooth. Add egg mixture and nuts. Bake at 325° for 20-25 minutes. Cool in pan. Yields two dozen. Recipe may be doubled.

Feeding the Faithful

Dessert Nut Butterhorns

DOUGH:

4 cups flour
1 teaspoon salt
1 package yeast, prepared
1 1/4 cups margarine

3 egg yolks, beaten
1 cup sour cream
1 teaspoon vanilla extract

Sift flour and salt. Add yeast and margarine with a pastry blender. Combine egg yolks, sour cream and vanilla. Stir in flour mixture. Knead until a smooth ball is formed. Divide dough into five portions. Chill for several hours.

FILLING:

3 egg whites, stiffly beaten
1 cup sugar

2 cups finely ground walnuts
1 teaspoon vanilla extract

Combine all ingredients. On a board sprinkled with powdered sugar, roll each portion of dough into a 12-inch circle. Cut into 12 wedges. Cover each wedge with filling; roll as a crescent roll. Place point down on a greased cookie sheet. Bake at 350° for 18-20 minutes. Yield: 60 servings.

Thoroughbred Fare

Christmas Tarts

2 eggs
1 cup sugar
1 stick butter
1 teaspoon vanilla

1 cup nuts, chopped
1 cup currants or cut
 raisins

Cream all ingredients together.

PASTRY MIX:

1 small package cream
 cheese

1 stick butter
1 1/2 cups flour

Mix and roll pastry thin. Mold into pastry cups. (Inverted small muffin tins work well.) Put 1 teaspoon filling into a pastry cup. Bake at 325° 15 minutes. Makes 20 tarts.

Southern Cooking

Sinful German Chocolate Squares

1 (14-ounce) bag of caramel
candies
2/3 cup evaporated milk,
divided
1 (18 1/2-ounce) package
German chocolate cake mix

3/4 cup of softened butter
1 cup chopped pecans
1 (6-ounce) package
semi-sweet chocolate chips

Preheat oven to 350°. Combine caramels and 1/3 cup of evaporated milk in top of double boiler. Heat, stirring constantly, until caramels are completely melted. Remove from heat and set aside. Combine cake mix, remaining 1/3 cup of evaporated milk and butter. Beat with electric mixer until mixture holds together. Stir in nuts. Press half of mixture into well-greased 9x13-inch baking pan. Bake for 6 minutes. Sprinkle chocolate chips over crust. Cover evenly with caramel mixture. Crumble remaining cake mixture on top of caramel layer. Bake 17-20 minutes. Cool. Chill for 30 minutes before cutting into small squares. Yield: 5 dozen.

Uptown Down South

Better Than Brownies

1/2 cup butter
5 tablespoons cocoa
1 egg
1/4 cup sugar
1 teaspoon vanilla

2 cups graham cracker
crumbs, or 1 1/2
cups prepackaged
1 cup coconut
1/2 cup chopped walnuts

FROSTING:
1/4 cup butter, softened
2 tablespoons instant
vanilla pudding mix

3 tablespoons milk
2 cups powdered sugar
1/2 teaspoon salt

Place first 5 ingredients in top of double boiler. Cook, stirring, until melted and thick. Add crumbs, coconut and walnuts, mixing well. Press mixture into an ungreased 8-inch square pan. Set aside. Cream together frosting ingredients in order given. Spread on top of crust. Refrigerate 15 minutes.

CONTINUED

CONTINUED

GLAZE:

4 (1-ounce) squares
  semi-sweet chocolate
1 tablespoon butter

1 (1-ounce) square
  unsweetened chocolate

Melt glaze ingredients in top of double boiler, stirring to blend. Spread over frosting. Refrigerate. Before serving, cut into bars with a sharp knife. Store in freezer. Yields 16.

Putting On The Grits

Hot Brownie with Fudge Sauce

This is the chocoholic's dream come true! You can even mix this in the same dish you are going to cook it in!

1 cup instant biscuit baking
  mix
1 cup sugar
3 tablespoons plus 1/3 cup
  cocoa

1/2 cup milk (you can use
  skim milk if you think it
  will help)
1 teaspoon vanilla
1 2/3 cups hot water

Mix biscuit mix, 1/2 cup sugar and 3 tablespoons cocoa in 8x8-inch glass baking dish. Stir in milk and vanilla until blended. Sprinkle with remaining 1/3 cup cocoa and 1/2 cup sugar. (Do not stir). Pour water over top and DO NOT STIR! Bake at 350° for 40 minutes. Top will look and taste like a brownie. Underneath is this heavenly chocolate syrup. Spoon in dessert dishes and top with whipped cream. This recipe should be outlawed! It is just not right to be this easy and taste so GOOD!

One Course At A Time

 A "Geechie" is a native of the South Caroloina coast.

Lemon Cream Cheese Bars

FIRST LAYER:

1 box lemon cake mix
  (Duncan Hines)
1 egg

1 stick margarine (room
  temperature)

Mix by hand and press in the bottom of a greased 9x13x2-inch pan.

SECOND LAYER:

1 (8-ounce) package cream
  cheese (room temperature)
3 cups powdered sugar

2 eggs
1 teaspoon vanilla
1 cup chopped nuts

Mix first four ingredients. This layer can be mixed with a mixer. Stir in 1 cup chopped nuts and spread over first layer. Bake 40 minutes at 350°. Sprinkle powdered sugar on top when taken from oven. Cool and cut into squares or bars.

Feeding the Faithful

Blondies
(Brown Sugar Cookie Bars)

3/4 cup shortening
2 1/2 cups brown sugar
3 eggs
2 3/4 cups flour
1/2 teaspoon salt

2 1/2 teaspoons baking
  powder
1 small package chocolate
  chips
1 cup nuts

Melt shortening and cool. Add brown sugar and eggs, beating with mixer until well blended. Sift flour, baking powder and salt. Add to sugar mixture, blending with mixer. Stir in chocolate chips and nuts. Pour into pan. Bake at 350° for 30 minutes. Cool 10 minutes. Cut in bars. Remove from pan with metal spatula. Yields 40-50 cookies.

Carolina Cuisine

No Bake Chocolate Cookies

2 cups sugar	3 cups raw quick rolled oats
1/2 cup milk	1 teaspoon vanilla
1 stick margarine	1/2 cup broken nuts
3 tablespoons cocoa	1 cup coconut (optional)
1 teaspoon salt	

Mix sugar, milk, margarine, cocoa, and salt in large saucepan and bring to a boil. Remove from heat and stir in the rolled oats, vanilla, nuts, and coconut. Drop from teaspoon onto waxed paper. Yields 48 cookies.

Carolina Cuisine

Yummy Peanut Butter Balls

1/2 cup honey
1 cup peanut butter
1 cup instant powdered milk

1/2 cup raisins
Coconut

Mix together all ingredients except coconut. Shape into balls.
Roll in the coconut and chill or freeze. Serves 4.

Please Don't Feed the Alligators

Butterscotch Drops

1 (12-ounce) package
  butterscotch chips
2 tablespoons peanut butter
1/2-1 cup slivered almonds,
  toasted

2 cups cornflakes
1/2 teaspoon vanilla
Dash salt

Melt butterscotch in the top of a double boiler. Add peanut
butter, and stir well. Add almonds, cornflakes, vanilla, and
salt. Drop by teaspoonful onto greased cookie sheet. Chill
until firm. Yields 4-6 dozen. May be frozen for 2 weeks.

Stir Crazy!

Energy Candy

1/4 cup molasses
1/4 cup honey
1/2 cup peanut butter
(natural, old-fashioned,
preferable)

1/2 cup seedless raisins
(optional)
1 cup powdered milk

Mix well in a bowl and form a ball. Add more powdered milk if necessary. Knead on a board until stiff. Cut into small squares and let stand for a few hours until hardened.

Culinary Crinkles

Granola

3 cups uncooked oatmeal
1 cup toasted wheat germ
1 cup unsweetened coconut
2 tablespoons cinnamon
2 tablespoons brown sugar

1/4 cup powdered milk
1/3 cup honey
1/3 cup vegetable oil
1 teaspoon vanilla extract

Mix dry ingredients together in a large glass dish. Combine honey, oil, and vanilla and heat. Pour warm liquid over dry ingredients using hands to mix. Place in oven at 300° for 30 minutes, stirring several times. Cool before storing in an airtight container. Serves 6.

Variation: Add after mixture has cooled: raisins, dates, nuts, seeds.

Please Don't Feed the Alligators

 The official state tree, the Palmetto, is on the state seal and the state flag. It is symbolic of the defeat of the British fleet by the fort on Sullivan's Island, built of Palmetto logs.

Divinity Fudge

3 cups brown sugar
  (dissolved in one cup of
  boiling water)
3/4 cup corn syrup (white)

2 stiffly beaten egg whites
1 teaspoon vinegar
1 cup chopped walnuts

Let sugar, water and syrup cook slowly until it strings. Pour on egg whites, to which the vinegar has been added. Beat until it is stiff enough to stand when dropped on a dish, add nuts and pour out.

Charleston Receipts

Pies and Desserts

Along the thickly wooded foothills of the Chattooga River on the Georgia border, white-water rafting is a popular sport. The river is well-known as the location for the filming of the movie, "Deliverance."

Lemon Chocolate Pie

1 (16-ounce) package semi-
  sweet chocolate chips
2 eggs
1/2 cup sugar
1/2 cup whipping cream
1/2 teaspoon vanilla
1 (9-inch) pie shell, baked
1/3 cup cornstarch

1 tablespoon grated lemon
  rind
1/4 teaspoon salt
2 cups water
2 egg yolks
1/3 cup lemon juice
1 cup sugar

Melt chocolate chips in top of a double boiler. Add eggs and
sugar, blending thoroughly, and cool completely. Whip cream
with vanilla until thick. Fold into chocolate and pour into baked
pie shell; refrigerate. In a saucepan, combine cornstarch, lemon
rind and salt. Gradually add water, mixing until smooth. In
a separate bowl, beat egg yolks and lemon juice until ivory in
color. Add sugar, beating well. Combine egg mixture with
cornstarch mixture and cook over medium heat, stirring constantly, until thick; cool. Spoon over chocolate layer. Refrigerate 4-6 hours before serving. Serves 6-8.

Putting On The Grits

Quakertown Crumb Pie

1/2 cup brown sugar
1/2 cup light Karo
1 egg

1 1/2 cups water
1 tablespoon flour
1 teaspoon vanilla

TOP PART:
1 cup flour
1/2 cup brown sugar

1/4 cup shortening (melted)
1/2 teaspoon soda

Combine 1/2 cup brown sugar, Karo, egg, water, 1 tablespoon
flour and vanilla in saucepan and bring to a boil till it thickens. Pour into an unbaked 9-inch pie shell. Add all the ingredients for the top part together and sprinkle on top. Bake
35-40 minutes at 375°.

500 Favorite Recipes

Buttermilk Custard Pie

3/4 cup butter
1/2 cup sugar (about)
3 eggs, separated
3 tablespoons flour

Grated rind of 1 lemon
2 cups buttermilk
Pastry

Cream the butter and sugar and add the well-beaten egg yolks. Add the flour, grated lemon rind and then the buttermilk. Fold in the stiffly beaten egg whites and turn into two pie pans lined with pastry. The crust should be baked in a hot oven for fifteen minutes before putting in the filling.

Bake in a moderately hot oven (375°) for about forty minutes. If the milk is very sour, add more sugar. We found that 2/3 cup sugar was needed when we tested this recipe.

Two Hundred Years of Charleston Cooking

No Crust Coconut Pie

3 eggs
1 1/2 cups sugar
2 tablespoons flour
1 large can evaporated milk
1 teaspoon vanilla

3/4 stick butter or
  margarine, melted
1 box or (3 1/2-ounce) can
  Angel Flake coconut

Beat eggs slightly. Add sugar and flour. Mix well and add milk, vanilla, margarine, and coconut. Pour into a well-greased and floured pan. Bake in a 375° oven for 30-35 minutes.

Note: Peach, pineapple or other fruit may be substituted for coconut.

Cooking on the Go

Mexican Dessert Turnovers

PASTRY:

1 (3-ounce) package cream
  cheese
1 cup sifted flour

1/4 pound butter or
  margarine

Mix all ingredients together until mixture holds together.
Divide dough in half and roll one half at a time on a lightly
floured board to thickness of regular pastry. Cut into circles
3 inches in diameter. (Chill dough before rolling if difficult to
handle.)

FILLING:

1/2 cup mashed sweet
  potatoes
1/2 cup drained crushed
  pineapple

1/4 cup sugar
1/4 teaspoon salt
1/4 cup flaked coconut

Mix all ingredients together thoroughly. Put a heaping teaspoonful of filling on one side of the pastry circle. Fold pastry
over filling to make a half-moon, and press edges together with
the tines of a fork. Transfer to a cookie sheet and bake 15
minutes or until golden brown at 375°.

Note: Excellent with coffee or tea.

Thoroughbred Fare

Dixie Sweet Potato Pie

PIE:

1 cup sweet potatoes, cooked
   and mashed
1 (12-ounce) can evaporated
   milk
1/2 cup margarine, melted
2 cups sugar

4 eggs
1 teaspoon nutmeg
1 teaspoon cinnamon
1 teaspoon vanilla
2 deep-dish pie shells,
   unbaked

TOPPING:

1 cup brown sugar
1 tablespoon margarine,
   melted

1 teaspoon vanilla
1 egg, well beaten

Preheat oven to 350°. With an electric mixer, combine all pie ingredients. Mix well. Pour into pie shells, and bake 30 minutes or until lightly browned. Combine all topping ingredients, and spread over pies. Return to oven until browned. Watch closely—topping will burn easily. Serves 16.

Stir Crazy!

Kahlua Pecan Pie

1 pie shell
1/4 cup butter
3/4 cup sugar
1 teaspoon vanilla
2 teaspoons flour

3 eggs
1/2 cup Kahlua
1/2 cup corn syrup
3/4 cup evaporated milk
1 cup chopped pecans

Set oven at 400°. Mix butter, sugar, vanilla and flour. Beat in eggs one at a time. Stir in Kahlua, corn syrup, evaporated milk and pecans, mix well. Pour into pie shell. Bake for 10 minutes then reduce heat to 325°. Continue cooking until firm, approximately 25 minutes. From the Player's Club.

Island Events Cookbook

Mrs. Strom Thurmond's Watermelon Pie

4 cups chopped watermelon rind
2 oranges, peeled and finely chopped
2 tablespoons lemon juice
1 teaspoon grated lemon rind
2 cups brown sugar
1/2 teaspoon ground nutmeg
1/2 teaspoon ground cinnamon
1/4 teaspoon curry powder
Dash cayenne pepper
1 (9-inch) pie shell, baked
1 cup crumbled gingersnaps
9 egg whites, beaten

Place watermelon rind in a large saucepan and barely cover with water. Bring to a boil and add oranges, lemon juice and lemon rind. Cook until watermelon is transparent. Stir in brown sugar and spices. Allow mixture to cool. Pour into pie shell and sprinkle with gingersnap crumbs. Spread beaten egg whites over top. Bake for 20 minutes at 325°. Serves 8. (Senator Strom Thurmond was elected United States Senator from South Carolina in 1954.)

Putting On The Grits

Tasty Pastries

1 package active dry yeast
1/4 cup warm water
2 sticks pie crust mix
1 tablespoon sugar
1 egg yolk
1/2 cup strawberry preserves
1 cup sifted confectioners' sugar
1-2 tablespoons milk
1 teaspoon vanilla

Dissolve yeast in warm water. Crumble pie crust mix into bowl. Stir in sugar, egg yolk and yeast; mix well. Roll dough into 3/4-inch balls. On baking sheet, shape into shells 1 1/4-inch in diameter and 1/4-inch deep. Spoon about 1/2 teaspoon preserves into each. Let rise in warm place for 1 hour. Bake at 375° for 15 minutes. Cool slightly; remove from baking sheet. Blend confectioners' sugar, milk and vanilla till smooth. Drizzle over pastries. Makes 3 dozen.

Cooking on the Go

Cranberry-Peach Pie

1 (29-ounce) can peach
  slices
3 cups fresh cranberries
1 1/2 cups sugar

3 tablespoons cornstarch
1/4 cup chopped toasted
  almonds
Pastry for double-crust pie

Drain peaches, reserving 1 cup syrup; coarsely cut up peaches and set aside. In saucepan combine cranberries and reserved peach syrup; cook 5-8 minutes or till skins of cranberries pop. Combine sugar and cornstarch. Stir into hot cranberries. Cook quickly, stirring constantly, till mixture is thickened and bubbly. Remove from heat. Stir in peaches and almonds; set aside to cool.

Pour peach mixture into pastry-lined 9-inch pie plate. Cut remaining pastry into 1/2-inch-wide strips. Weave strips atop filling to make lattice crust; flute edge. To prevent over-browning, cover edge of pie with foil. Bake at 375° for 20 minutes. Remove foil; bake for 20-25 minutes more. Cool on rack before serving.

The Peach Sampler

Easy Blueberry (or Cherry) Dessert

1 can blueberry or cherry
  pie filling
1 can crushed pineapple
  (and juice)

1 box yellow cake mix
1 (4-ounce) package coconut
1 pound pecans
1 cup melted butter

Layer the above ingredients (except butter) in a 9x13-inch baking pan. Pour melted butter over top and bake at 350° for 1 hour.

Thoroughbred Fare

In the courthouse square in Barnwell stands a 155-year-old Vertical Sundial. Believed to be the only one of its kind in the country, it keeps perfect time.

Blackberry Cobbler

1 cup sugar
2 cups blackberries*
1 stick butter or margarine,
  softened

1 1/4 cups Bisquick
1 1/4 cups milk

Mix 1/4 cup of sugar with berries and set aside. Mix remaining sugar and other ingredients together, and pour into a well greased baking dish. Spoon berry-sugar mixture on top but do not stir. Bake at 350° until golden brown—about 45 minutes.

   *Other berries or fruits may be used—adjust amount of sugar according to taste.

Stirrin' The Pots On Daufuskie

Pawleys Island Cobbler

1/4 cup butter
1/2 cup sugar
1/2 cup milk
1 cup sifted flour

2 teaspoons baking powder
1/4 teaspoon salt
Fruit and juice*
Sugar

Cream butter and sugar; add milk and dry ingredients. Pour batter into a 2-quart greased casserole. Place fruit, sugar, and juice over batter in that order. Bake at 375° for 45 minutes or until batter rises to top, browns, and cobbler is bubbly.

   *For filling, use enough fresh fruit of any kind, sugared, to cover bottom of 2-quart casserole or No. 2 can of cherries, blackberries, etc. If using canned fruit, use 1/4 cup sugar and 1 cup of juice.

Feeding the Faithful

The many wax myrtle shrubs that flourished in the sandy soil in 1900 were cause for the area being named Myrtle Beach. Its warm climate, clean ocean water, and white sandy beaches have made it one the best beach resorts in the world.

Strawberry Delight

CRUST:
2 cups pretzels, crushed   3/4 cup margarine, melted
3 tablespoons sugar

Mix well. Bake in 9x13-inch pan 8 minutes at 400°. Cool.

SECOND LAYER:
1 (8-ounce) package cream   2 cups Cool Whip
  cheese   1 cup sugar

Mix well and spread over cooled crust.

THIRD LAYER:
1 (6-ounce) package   2 cups boiling water
  strawberry Jello
2 (10-ounce) packages frozen
  strawberries

Combine and place in refrigerator until partially congealed. Spread over second layer. Refrigerate several hours, cut in squares.

Cooking on the Go

Blueberry Delight

1 1/4 sticks butter   3 tablespoons milk
2 tablespoons sugar   1 - 1 1/2 cups chopped
2 cups graham cracker   pecans
  crumbs   1 can blueberry pie filling
1 cup confectioners' sugar   1 giant carton Cool Whip
1 (8-ounce) package cream
  cheese

Melt butter and add sugar and crumbs. Press into 9x13-inch pan and bake at 350° for 8 minutes. Cool. Whip confectioners' sugar, cream cheese and milk until smooth. Spread on cooled crust. Sprinkle with nuts and then spread blueberry pie filling on top of nuts. Top with Cool Whip. Chill thoroughly.

Carolina Cuisine Encore!

Chocolate Éclairs

PASTRY:

1 cup water
1 stick oleo
1 cup sifted flour
4 eggs

Heat water and oleo to boiling point. Add flour and stir constantly until mixture forms a ball. Remove from heat and let cool. Beat in eggs one at a time. Drop dough from teaspoon to form small éclairs on ungreased cookie sheet. Cook at 400° for 30 minutes or until lightly browned. Cool slowly away from draft.

FILLING:

3 cups rich milk
3/4 cup sugar
1/2 teaspoon salt
6 tablespoons flour
3 whole eggs
2 teaspoons vanilla

Combine milk, sugar, salt and flour. Cook slowly until thick. Add beaten eggs and cook until even thicker. When cool, add vanilla. Cut off the tops of puffs and add the custard mixture. Replace tops.

ICING:

2 (1-ounce) squares baking
   chocolate
2 cups sugar
1 cup cream

Melt chocolate; add sugar and cream. Cook over medium heat until soft ball stage is reached. Cool, then beat. Put icing on the éclairs. Yields 12 large éclairs or 60-70 miniature éclairs.

Carolina Cuisine

The Cornerstone Inc.'s Banana Éclair

HOT FUDGE SAUCE:

2 squares unsweetened
 baking chocolate
1/3 cup butter or margarine

4 tablespoons sugar
1 cup heavy cream
2 teaspoons vanilla extract

Melt chocolate and butter over low heat, stirring to blend. Add sugar and stir until completely dissolved. Add heavy cream, stirring to combine. Remove from heat. Add vanilla and stir until well mixed. Set aside.

ÉCLAIR:

4 commercial croissants
2 sliced bananas
1 (3-ounce) package vanilla
 pudding (follow package
 directions)

Split croissants and evenly divide sliced bananas among each pocket. Spoon in desired amount of vanilla pudding, and drizzle Hot Fudge Sauce over top. Serves 4.

South Carolina's Historic Restaurants

The Greenhouse Restaurant's
Fried Bananas

1 banana
1/2 cup self-rising flour
1 cup cooking oil or fat
1/4 cup honey

1 teaspoon mayonnaise
1/4 teaspoon cinnamon
1/4 cup finely chopped
 pecans

Peel the banana and cut lengthwise into four sections. Roll each section in flour. Fry in hot oil until golden brown; drain. Combine honey, mayonnaise and cinnamon, mixing well so flavors are thoroughly blended. Pour honey sauce over ba-nanas and sprinkle with pecans. Serves 1 or 2.

South Carolina's Historic Restaurants

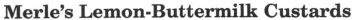

Merle's Lemon-Buttermilk Custards

3/4 cup sugar
3 tablespoons cornstarch
1 1/2 cups buttermilk
2 tablespoons butter or
  margarine

3 eggs, separated
1 1/2 teaspoons lemon rind
1/4 cup lemon juice
1/4 cup sugar
Lemon twists

Preheat oven to 400°. Combine 3/4 cup sugar and cornstarch in a heavy saucepan; stir well. Add buttermilk and cook over heat, stirring constantly until thickened. Stir in butter. Combine egg yolks, lemon rind and lemon juice; beat well.

Gradually stir in about a fourth of hot mixture into yolks; add remaining hot mixture, stirring constantly. Cook, stirring constantly, over low heat for 4 minutes or until smooth and thickened. Spoon mixture into four 10-ounce ungreased custard cups. Beat egg whites (at room temperature) in large bowl at high speed with electric mixer until foamy. Gradually add 1/4 cup sugar, 1 tablespoon at a time, beating until stiff peaks form. Spread meringue over custards. Make sure all edges are sealed. Garnish with lemon twists. Yield: 4 servings.

Years ago when thick, slightly tart buttermilk was the by-product of churning butter from milk, thrifty Southerners soon found ways to use it. This recipe uses the buttermilk taste in that old fashioned tradition.

Per Serving: Calories 352; Protein 8 g; Cholesterol 224 mg; Fiber .1g
Percent of Calories: Protein 8%; Carbohydrates 65%; Fat 26%

Palmetto Evenings

Huckleberry Pudding

By using well-drained canned huckleberries in place of the fresh ones, this pudding may be made the year around.

1/4 cup butter	4 teaspoons baking powder
1 cup sugar	1 cup milk
2 eggs	2 cups huckleberries
1 1/2 cups flour	

Cream the butter and sugar and add the beaten eggs. Dredge the berries with part of the flour. Sift together the flour and baking powder and add to the first mixture alternately with the milk. Stir the berries into the dough and pour into a well-buttered baking dish. Bake in a moderate oven (350°) for about forty-five minutes. Serve with hard sauce.

Two Hundred Years of Charleston Cooking

Cheesecake Cousin

Non-caloric sweetener	Graham cracker crumbs
Vanilla	Melted butter
Small curd cottage cheese	Cinnamon
Fresh peach halves	

Stir non-caloric sweetener and a dash of vanilla into small curd cottage cheese. Spoon into the center of fresh peach halves. Sprinkle with graham cracker crumbs mixed with a little melted butter and a dash of cinnamon. Cheesecake goodness without the calories!

The Peach Sampler

Rice Pudding

2 eggs
2 cups whole milk
1 1/4 cups cold, cooked rice
1 cup seedless raisins

1/2 cup sugar
1/4 teaspoon salt
1 teaspoon vanilla extract
Dash nutmeg

Beat eggs until light and thick and add to the milk in mixing bowl. Blend in remaining ingredients and place in a lightly buttered 1 1/2-quart casserole dish. Bake in shallow pan of water at 350° one hour, or until mixture is firm. Serves 6.

Southern Vegetable Cooking

Pineapple Charlotte Russe

2 tablespoons gelatin
2 cups sweet milk
1 pint whipping cream
2 egg whites

1 cup sugar
1 medium-sized can
  pineapple, drained

Dissolve gelatin in 1/2 cup milk. Bring 1 1/2 cups milk to boiling point. Mix hot milk with dissolved gelatin. Let cool. Whip cream and whites of eggs, then add milk and gelatin, whipping constantly. Then add sugar and pineapple. Rinse mold with cold water. Pour mixture into mold. Store in refrigerator until congealed. I vary this—sometimes I use orange pulp, same amount as pineapple.

The South Carolina Cook Book

Chocolate Mousse

You will not see this recipe version for the chocoholics' delight anywhere. It was perfected by my chef friend John Bennett. The chocolate base should be made the day before you plan to serve the mousse.

1 pound semi-sweet chocolate, plus 2 ounces for grating	**1/4 cup water**
	1/2 cup egg yolks
	1 cup egg whites
1 stick (1/4-pound) unsalted butter	**1/4 teaspoon cream of tartar**
	1 pint heavy cream
1 cup superfine sugar	
6 tablespoons light Karo syrup	

Melt the chocolate and butter in a double boiler. Keep warm. In a heavy-bottomed, uncovered pot, prepare a syrup of the sugar, Karo syrup, and water. Place over moderate heat until it forms an 8-inch thread* (this will take approximately 15-25 minutes).

While the syrup is boiling, whip the egg yolks at high speed with an electric mixer until ribbons are formed (about 10-15 minutes). Reduce the mixer to low speed while pouring in the hot syrup in a thin stream. Continue to beat while adding the chocolate mixture in small amounts until all is incorporated. Transfer this base into a large bowl and let cool to room temperature (about 1 hour).

In a clean bowl, beat the egg whites with the cream of tartar at high speed until stiff, moist peaks are formed. Carefully fold this into the chocolate base with a rubber spatula. Refrigerate for at least 6 hours or overnight.

Beat the cream until very stiff and fold half of it into the chilled mousse. Place this in a serving bowl and decorate with the extra whipped cream and grated semi-sweet chocolate. Refrigerate for another 6 hours before serving. Yield: 8 servings.

*A wooden spoon lowered into the syrup and then held 8 inches above the surface will cause an unbroken thread of syrup to form when the proper temperature is reached. Keep testing until the thread is formed. If you are using a candy thermometer, the syrup needs to reach 234°.

A Journal of Fine Cooking

Easy Chocolate Mint Mousse

1 (6-ounce) package
  chocolate covered mints
1 (6-ounce) package
  semi-sweet chocolate chips

1/3 cup sugar
3 eggs
1 cup milk
1 cup whipping cream

Place mints, chips, sugar and eggs in blender. Scald milk. Add hot milk slowly to blender. Blend until smooth. Pour into bowl. Chill until it begins to set. Whip cream and fold into chocolate mixture. Spoon into sherbet dishes and chill until set. This is very rich. Yield: 8-10 servings.

Prescriptions for Good Eating

Orange Bavarian Cream

2 envelopes unflavored
  gelatine
1 cup orange juice
1 cup boiling water
2 cups orange juice

Juice of 1/2 lemon
3/4 cup sugar
2 cups whipping cream,
  whipped

Soften gelatine in 1 cup orange juice. Add boiling water to dissolve. Then add 2 cups orange juice, lemon juice, and sugar. Mix well and let cool. When cold, fold in whipped cream. Pour into glass bowl, mold, or individual cups or molds. Chill. Serves 8.

Nell Graydon's Cook Book

 Poinsett State Park is named after a Sumter native, Joel Poinsett, who introduced the Poinsetta flower to the United States and served as U.S. Ambassador to Mexico in the 1800's.

Lemon Mousse "Eggs"
with Raspberry Sauce

MOUSSE:

2 1/2 teaspoons unflavored
  gelatin
3/4 cup sugar
1/4 cup fresh lemon juice

1 teaspoon grated lemon rind
3 egg whites
Pinch cream of tartar

In large bowl, sprinkle gelatin over 1/4 cup cold water and let set 10 minutes until softened. Add 1 cup boiling water and 1/2 cup sugar, stirring until sugar dissolves. Stir in lemon juice and rind. Chill mixture for 1 hour or until just begins to set. Beat with electric mixer until light and frothy. In separate bowl, beat egg whites until stiff with a pinch of cream of tartar and remaining 1/4 cup sugar until they will hold soft peaks. Stir meringue gently into lemon mixture and chill mousse covered 1 hour or until set.

SAUCE:

3 (10-ounce) packages frozen
  raspberries, thawed and
  drained
1 1/2 tablespoons sugar

3 tablespoons heavy cream
Fresh raspberries or mint
  for garnish

Purée in food processor raspberries, sugar, and cream. Force mixture through sieve into bowl. Divide sauce among 6 chilled plates, using a soup spoon to make 3 "eggs" on each plate. Add garnish. Serves 6.

Charleston Receipts Repeats

Frozen Chocolate Charlotte

1/2 cup white créme de
  menthe
Ladyfingers
1 (8-ounce) package
  semi-sweet chocolate
6 egg yolks, beaten

1/2 cup sugar
3 tablespoons instant coffee
1/2 cup boiling water
1 teaspoon vanilla
6 egg whites, beaten
1 1/2 cups whipped cream

Brush surface of 9-inch spring mold with créme de menthe
and then line mold with ladyfingers. Melt chocolate in top of
double boiler. Beat egg yolks in bowl until foamy. Beat in
sugar gradually and beat until thick. Dissolve coffee in boiling water. Add coffee, vanilla, and chocolate to egg yolks and
sugar. Beat egg whites until stiff. Stir 1 cup egg whites into
chocolate to lighten it. Fold in whipped cream which has been
blended with rest of egg whites. Serves 12.

Sea Island Seasons

Pralines and Cream

1/2 cup oatmeal
1/2 cup brown sugar
1 cup butter, softened
1 cup chopped pecans
2 cups sifted flour

2 (12-ounce) jars caramel
  ice cream topping, divided
1/2 gallon vanilla ice
  cream, softened

Mix together oatmeal, brown sugar, butter, pecans and flour.
Spread in a 9x15-inch pan. Bake for 20 minutes at 350°, stirring every 5 minutes to keep crumbled. Divide in half. Spread
half the mixture in an ungreased 9x15-inch pan. Pour one
jar caramel topping over crumbs. Pack softened ice cream on
top. Pour second jar caramel topping over ice cream. Sprinkle
remaining crumbs on top. Freeze. When ready to serve, cut
into squares. Store in freezer. Serves 15.

Putting On The Grits

Coffee Sundae Pie

1 package Nabisco chocolate
  refrigerator cookies
2/3 cup melted butter or
  margarine
3 squares unsweetened
  chocolate
1 cup sugar

2 tablespoons butter or
  margarine
2 small cans evaporated milk
1/2 gallon coffee ice cream
1/2 pint whipping cream
Chopped pecans

Crush cookies into fine crumbs. Divide into 2 small pie plates. Add 1/3 cup melted butter to each plate. Mix crumbs and butter well. Press around sides and on bottom to make crusts. Put in freezer. Melt chocolate over hot water and stir in sugar and 2 tablespoons butter. Add evaporated milk very slowly. Stir occasionally until thickened. When thick, chill until quite thick. (It is important that this chocolate sauce be quite thick.) Fill shells with coffee ice cream. Spread chocolate sauce on top. Top with whipped cream and chopped nuts. One pie serves 6-8.

The Museum Cookbook

Gold Eagle Benne Delight

1/2 cup butter
1 cup evaporated milk
1 (16-ounce) box light brown
  sugar

1 cup marshmallows
Benne seed, toasted

Combine butter, evaporated milk, brown sugar and marshmallows in double boiler. Cook until soft and marshmallows are melted. Store in refrigerator in jar and reheat as needed. Serve hot on vanilla ice cream with benne seed sprinkled over the top. Makes 1 quart.

Sea Island Seasons

Carolina Trifle

1/2 (9-inch) cake layer
3/4 cup grated coconut
1 (3 3/4-ounce) package
  instant vanilla pudding
3 cups milk
1 teaspoon vanilla

1 (3-ounce) package Dream
  Whip
1/2 cup milk
1/2 teaspoon vanilla
2 - 3 tablespoons powdered
  sugar

Crumble cake and place one-half in 6x10-inch casserole. Sprinkle with 1/4 cup coconut. Make the pudding by directions using 3 cups milk and 1 teaspoon vanilla. Quickly pour one-half pudding over the cake and coconut. Add the remaining cake and 1/4 cup coconut and the remaining pudding. Top with the Dream Whip that has been made with the milk, vanilla, and powdered sugar. Sprinkle with the remaining coconut. Refrigerate at least 3 hours and serve very cold. Serves 8-10.

Sea Island Seasons

Index

One of South Carolina's many marshes and inlets. Sometimes called
the nursery of the sea, they team with fish and crabs.

INDEX

INDEX

INDEX

Railroad philanthropist, Archer Huntington and his wife Anna Hyatt Huntington discovered Brookgreen Plantation during a visit to Georgetown County in 1930. The couple purchased Brookgreen along with three adjoining properties, the Oaks, Laurel Hill and Springfield plantations. Today, Brookgreen Gardens, accredited by the American Association of Zoological Parks and Aquariums, encompasses 9,000 acres.

Catalog of
Contributing
Cookbooks

The nation's largest collection of statuary in an outdoor setting is at South Carolina's Brookgreen Gardens near Myrtle Beach.

CATALOG OF CONTRIBUTING COOKBOOKS

All recipes in this book have been submitted from the South Carolina cookbooks shown on the following pages. Individuals who wish to obtain a copy of any particular book can do so by sending a check or money order to the addresses listed. Prices are subject to change. Please note the postage and handling charges that are required. South Carolina residents add tax only when requested. Retailers are invited to call or write to same address for wholesale information.

BETHEL FOOD BAZAAR II

BETHEL UNITED METHODIST CHURCH
SPARTANBURG, SOUTH CAROLINA

BETHEL FOOD BAZAAR II

Bethel United Methodist Women
245 South Church Street
Spartanburg, SC 29302   803/585-4801

Bethel Food Bazaar II is the second collection of favorite recipes from the women of the church. Bethel Food Bazaar I was published in 1974. The book contains 220 pages with 475 recipes, complete index and dedication page. The name was a result of many years of bazaars and covered dish luncheons featuring all kinds of good food.

$ 7.00 Retail price
$ 3.00 Postage and handling
Make check payable to Bethel United Methodist Women

BLUFFTON'S
FAVORITE
RECIPES

THE WOMEN OF THE CHURCH OF THE CROSS
Bluffton, S. C.

BLUFFTON'S FAVORITE RECIPES

The Women of the Church of the Cross
Box 146
Bluffton, SC 29910   803/757-2661

The handsome Church of the Cross overlooking the May River in the village of Bluffton was established in 1699 by a group of Londoners who sent missionaries to the Low Country to hold services for the plantation owners and their slaves. It is in the National Archives of Historical Churches. This cookbook of delicious member recipes helps support it.

$ 5.00 Retail price
$ .58 Tax for South Carolina residents
$ 1.50 Postage and handling
Make check payable to The Women of the Church of the Cross

CAROLINA CUISINE

The Junior Assembly of Anderson, SC
P. O. Box 931
Anderson, SC 29622

Carolina Cuisine contains 320 pages with more than 600 recipes which represent the finest in Southern cuisine and hospitality. Sections range from Appetizers to Desserts with special sections of menus, cooking for two, antique recipes, and cooking hints. *Carolina Cuisine* is a unique treasure in Southern cooking tradition.

$ 10.95 Retail price
$ .55 Tax for South Carolina residents
$ 1.25 Postage and handling
Make check payable to The Junior Assembly of Anderson, SC
ISBN 0-9617963-0-8

CAROLINA CUISINE ENCORE!

The Junior Assembly of Anderson, SC
P. O. Box 931
Anderson, SC 29622

Carolina Cuisine Encore! is filled with more than 600 Southern and contemporary recipes. Within 320 pages, there are many local favorites, delicious foreign recipes, and "New Trends in Cooking," an exciting section which includes recipes for the microwave, slow cooker, and food processor. Let *Encore!* become a familiar part of your kitchen!

$ 10.95 Retail price
$ .55 Tax for South Carolina residents
$ 1.25 Postage and handling
Make check payable to The Junior Assembly of Anderson, SC
ISBN 0-9617963-1-6

CATCH-OF-THE-DAY...
SOUTHERN SEAFOOD SECRETS

by Ginny Lentz (formerly a South Carolinian)
191 Hayes Run
Marshall, NC 28753   704/649-3339

Over 60,000 sold! · More than 150 easy recipes plus 17 menus · Appetizers, salads, sauces, stews, soups, chowders, main, side dishes, index · Hints on preparing, serving and stretching recipes · Tips on nutrition, selection, cleaning, and freezing · Microwave and "No-Thaw Cooking" techniques · Illustrated Seafood Appendix · A real buy for this price!

$ 8.95 Retail price
$ .45 Tax for North Carolina residents
$ 1.50 Postage and handling
Make check payable to *Catch-of-the-Day*
ISBN 0-88742-058-3

271

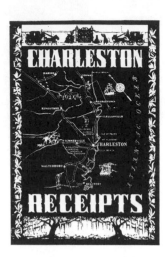

CHARLESTON RECEIPTS

The Junior League of Charleston, Inc.
51 Folly Road
Charleston, SC 29407   803/763-5284

Charleston Receipts celebrates its 40th anniversary this year and is heralded as a classic in the cookbook world. Many of the 700 recipes it contains are cherished from Charleston and neighboring plantations. *Charleston Receipts* preserves and blends the colorful past of the Lowcountry's art and history throughout its 376 pages.

$ 12.00 Retail price
$ .60 Tax for South Carolina residents
$ 2.00 Postage and handling
Make checks payable to *Charleston Receipts*
ISBN 0-9607854-2-6

CHARLESTON RECEIPTS REPEATS

The Junior League of Charleston, Inc.
51 Folly Road
Charleston, SC 29407   803/763-5284

This collection of over 600 recipes adds a new dimension to Lowcountry cookbooks and celebrates an abundance of fresh seafood and game, garden-grown vegetables and succulent fruits. *Charleston Receipts Repeats'* 372 pages reflect the sophisticated elegance that has marked Charleston through its 300-year history.

$ 14.95 Retail price
$ .75 Tax for South Carolina residents
$ 2.00 Postage and handling
Make check payable to *Charleston Receipts*
ISBN 0-9607854-5-0

CHARLESTON RECOLLECTIONS AND RECEIPTS:
ROSE P. RAVENEL'S COOKBOOK

University of South Carolina Press
1716 College Street
Columbia, SC 29208   803/777-5243

Rose P. Ravenel (1850-1943) was the daughter of a Huguenot planter, merchant and ship owner in Charleston. During her lifetime, she collected more than 200 recipes from Charleston ladies. This book contains 65 of her favorite Charleston recipes. Her memories of the famous Port City before and after the Civil War are included. 125 pages, clothbound.

$ 14.95 Retail price
$ .75 Tax for South Carolina residents
$ 2.00 Postage and handling
Make check payable to University of South Carolina Press
ISBN 0-87249-647-3

COOKING DONE THE BAPTIST WAY

The First Baptist Church
215 N. Main Street
Abbeville, SC 29620   803/459-2597

This cookbook is a collection of recipes submitted by the men, women and children of First Baptist Abbeville. The primary purpose of this endeavor is to help underwrite the expenses of our summer youth mission tours.

$ 5.00 Retail price
$ .25 Tax for South Carolina residents
$ 1.75 Postage and handling
Make check payable to First Baptist Abbeville

COOKING ON THE GO

by Nancy Welch
101 Summit Drive
Greer, SC 29651   803/877-5308

Recipes have come from viewers of my television show which I did for 21 years. All are quick and easy and designed to get you in and out of the kitchen so you can be "On the Go" again. Recipes have been tested to meet the approval of the busy working women of the 1990s. 137 pages, 400 recipes.

$ 7.00 Retail price
$ .35 Tax for South Carolina residents
$ 1.00 Postage and handling
Make check payable to NTW Enterprises

CULINARY CRINKLES

Presbyterian Women
East Cambridge Avenue/P.O. Box 426
Greenwood, SC 29646   803/229-5814

In 1908, the women of First Presbyterian Church first published and sold a cookbook, *Culinary Crinkles*, to help fund church needs. Since then, the book has been revised six times, increasing in size to a present 800 recipes, 312-page book, featuring the best local culinary skills. A very popular cookbook.

$ 7.50 Retail price
$ .38 Tax for South Carolina residents
$ 1.50 Postage and handling
Make check payable to Presbyterian Women

273

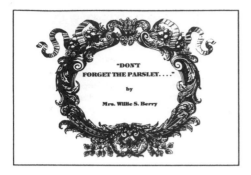

"DON'T FORGET THE PARSLEY..."

Orangeburg-Calhoun Technical
College Foundation
3240 St. Matthews Road, NE
Orangeburg, SC 29115   803/536-0311

Southern food . . . fresh vegetables, sea-food, homemade breads and pastries. Recipes by "Miss Willie," whose restaurant was known and loved from Maine to Florida, with dear friends' recipes as an added treat.

$ 5.95 Retail price
$ 1.50 Postage and handling
Make check payable to O-C Tech Foundation

THE ENLIGHTENED GOURMET

by Ann Cotton, Henrietta Gaillard
and Jo Anne Willis, R. D.
CGW Enterprises
P.O. Box 181
Charleston, SC 29402

The Enlightened Gourmet is a 256-page cookbook which presents a new approach for the cook who is not only interested in preparing good meals, but is also aware of the importance of a nutritionally sound diet. It supplies exciting recipes and a nutra-analysis system which informs you on a per-serving basis.

$ 9.95 Retail price
$ .55 Tax for South Carolina residents
$ 1.50 Postage and handling
Make check payable to CGW Enterprises

FEEDING THE FAITHFUL

United Methodist Women of
Mauldin United Methodist Church
100 East Butler Ave.
Mauldin, SC 29662   803/288-4728

"Feeding the Faithful" was compiled in 1983 to commemorate the 200th year of Methodism. In it you will find over 250 recipes from the kitchens of some of South Carolina's best cooks. Your special attention is called to the Heirloom Section where you will find such recipes as Homemade Mayonnaise, Chicken and Dumplings, Keepsake Biscuits, as well as homemade soap!

$ 8.50 Retail price
$ .43 Tax for South Carolina residents
$ 1.25 Postage and handling
Make check payable to Mauldin United Methodist Women

500 FAVORITE RECIPES

The Ladies of Whispering Pines
Mennonite Church
Route 1 Box 132B
Honea Path, SC 29654   803/369-0932

The Mennonite ladies are well known for being some
of the finest cooks. Among these recipes are some of
Grandma's old favorites. This unique book contains
500 recipes, colorful divider pages and over 400 help-
ful household hints. Wirebound, laminated cover,
165 pages.

$ 6.00 Retail price
$ 2.00 Postage and handling
Make check payable to Ada Chupp

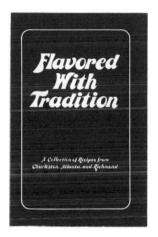

FLAVORED WITH TRADITION

P.O. Box 597
Johns Island, SC 29455   803/768-1321

Flavored With Tradition is a collection of favorite
recipes from Charleston, Atlanta, and Richmond, as
well as additions from other cities. The recipes are
both easy and delicious, often using many things
always found on your kitchen shelf. *Flavored With
Tradition* is truly for the novice as well as the gourmet cook. 224 pages.

$ 7.95 Retail price
$ .40 Tax for South Carolina residents
$ 1.25 Postage and handling
Make check payable to *Flavored With Tradition*

HUDSON'S COOKBOOK

Hudson's Seafood House
Hudson Road/P.O. Box 1056
Hilton Head Island, SC 29925   803/681-2773

This cookbook is a combined effort of many folks,
including all the management and staff at Hudson's
Seafood House, who have contributed, along with
the recipes, some interesting and colorful tidbits
about Hilton Head Island and the South Carolina
Low Country—all of which add valuable flavor to the
book. 172 pages, ringbound, fourth printing.

$ 8.95 Retail price
$ .40 Tax for South Carolina residents
$ 1.50 Postage and handling
Make check payable to Hudson's Seafood House

ISLAND EVENTS COOKBOOK

Edited by Jolie Donnell
P.O. Box 715
Telluride, CO 81435   303/728-6500 or 728-3063

Island Events Cookbook, an all new edition that includes sixteen years of prized recipes from *Island Events Magazine* and a wealth of "priceless" meal ideas from Hilton Head Island's leading restaurants, plus many facts and photos on the Island itself!

$ 8.95 Retail price
$ .45 Tax for South Carolina residents
$ 1.50 Postage and handling
Make check payable to *Island Events Cookbook*

A JOURNAL OF FINE COOKING

by Robert Dickson—Robert's of Charleston
112 N. Market
Charleston, SC 29401   803/577-7565

A collection of some of Chef Robert Dickson's favorite recipes including many from his world-famous restaurant, Robert's of Charleston. 150 pages hardbound with interior spiral to stay open while cooking.

$ 19.05 Retail price
$ .95 Tax for South Carolina residents
Make check payable to Robert's of Charleston

THE MUSEUM COOKBOOK

The Museum (Greenwood)
P.O. Box 3131/106 Main St.
Greenwood, SC 29648   803/229-7093

This cookbook features art work by two prominent local artists and by art students of Greenwood's Lander College. It contains 190 recipes, many of which are devoted to game such as pheasant and quail. The ninety pages are crammed full of (un)usual recipes (some 100 years old), sketches of artifacts on exhibit at The Museum, and advice on table etiquette from a 1907 cookbook.

$ 6.95 Retail price
$ .35 Tax for South Carolina residents
$ 1.25 Postage and handling
Make check payable to The Museum

NELL GRAYDON'S COOK BOOK: FROM MY HOUSE TO YOUR HOUSE

Sandlapper Publishing, Co., Inc.
P. O. Box 1932
Orangeburg, SC 29115   800/277-1673

This personalized cookbook contains many old recipes copied from friends and relatives, cookbooks, newspapers, and magazines during sixty years of the author's marriage. Reflecting upon her days as an inexperienced, young housewife to her abilities as an accomplished entertainer, the author provides both old and new ways of preparing food.

$ 11.95 Retail price
$ .60 Tax for South Carolina residents
$ 1.25 Postage and handling
Make check payable to Sandlapper Publishing Co., Inc.
ISBN 0-87844-057-7

OLIVIA'S FAVORITE MENUS AND RECIPES

by Olivia H. Adams
103 Bradley Boulevard
Greenville, SC 29609   803/244-5838

Over the years, my friends and family had this common complaint, "What can I cook for supper?" The menu format was born and has been used in my cookbook as a cook's aid in planning interesting as well as nutritionally balanced meals. And cooks love it! 204 pages, 549 recipes.

$ 9.95 Retail price
$ 1.25 Postage and handling
Make check payable to Olivia H. Adams

ONE COURSE AT A TIME

by Paddi B. Childers
2703 Duffy Street
N. Myrtle Beach. SC 29582   803/249-4845

Golf course goodies, family favorites and over 50 recipes from area restaurants and chefs. These 400 recipes span the culinary world of the Grand Strand from the glamorous ocean front resorts to the natives of Little River Neck. A must for cookbook collectors!

$ 9.95 Retail price
$ .50 Tax for South Carolina residents
$ 1.50 Postage and handling
Make check payable to *One Course at a Time*

PALMETTO EVENINGS

American Cancer Society/South Carolina Division
128 Stonemark Lane
Columbia, SC 29210   803/750-1693

Palmetto Evenings features 155 pages containing over 300 South Carolina recipes. Each recipe contains nutritional information about the dish. The cover and dividers are evening scenes of South Carolina which capture the special flavor of our state.

$ 10.00 Retail price
$ 1.50 Postage and handling
Make check payable to The American Cancer Society

THE PEACH SAMPLER

by Eliza Mears Horton
329 Corine Drive
West Columbia, SC 29169

A peach of an idea blossomed into full bloom! The attractively developed peach specialty cookbook entitled *The Peach Sampler* with its full four-color cover has 200 pages, 300-plus recipes, and a colorful spiral binding which allows it to lay flat. It contains a history of the peach, hints on selecting and utilizing peaches, tips on cooking and preserving peaches, and much, much more.

$ 9.95 Retail price
$ .50 Tax for South Carolina residents
$ 2.00 Postage and handling
Make check payable to At Home Enterprises
ISBN 0-960-99660-5

PLEASE DON'T FEED THE ALLIGATORS

Hilton Head Elementary School PTA
25 School Road
Hilton Head Island, SC 29928   803/681-2053

A collection of favorite recipes from Islanders and Restaurants. We do not claim that they are original, but they are favorites of our contributors. 538 recipes.

$ 10.95 Retail price
$ .58 Tax for South Carolina residents
$ 1.50 Postage and handling
ISBN 0-915726-0-4
Make check payable to Hilton Head Elementary PTA

POOL BAR JIM'S FAMOUS FROZEN DRINKS

by James D. Lisenby
P. O. Box 4958
Hilton Head Island, SC 29938   803/842-5314

"This book is a collection of what I consider the most fantastic recipes for frozen cocktails ever compiled. Each recipe will explain how, how much, why and a lot of other questions about aspects of frozen drinks you probably wouldn't think about." Includes techniques, measurements, party suggestions, etc. 166 pages, ringbound.

$ 6.95 Retail price
$ .28 Tax for South Carolina residents
$ 1.00 Postage and handling
Make check payable to *Pool Bar Jim's*

PRESCRIPTIONS FOR GOOD EATING

Greenville County Medical Society Auxiliary
P.O. Box 9254
Greenville, SC 29605-9254   803/233-3205

A collection of favorite recipes that have been thoroughly tested and edited. A special "Kitchen Aids" section includes: Cooking with herbs, Cooking with seeds, Cooking with spices, Cooking with wine and liqueurs, and definitions of cooking terms, measures and equivalents. The book includes 290 pages and 400 mouth-watering recipes.

$ 11.95 Retail price
$ .60 Tax for South Carolina residents
$ 1.50 Postage and handling
Make check payable to *Prescriptions for Good Eating*
ISBN 0-913679-0-3

PUTTING ON THE GRITS

The Junior League of Columbia, Inc.
3612 Landmark Drive, Suite A
Columbia, SC 29204   803/782-4833

Putting On The Grits brings you the best selection of our regional favorites. Over 300 pages and over 500 recipes, some time-honored, some new, reflect the traditions celebrated from coastal inlets to game-abounding woodlands. Don't miss the beautiful illustrations of South Carolina artist, Martha Elizabeth Ferguson, entertaining menus, and "Southern Classics" section.

$ 13.95 Retail price
$ .70 Tax for South Carolina residents
$ 1.75 Postage and handling
Make check payable to JLC Cookbook
ISBN 0-9613561-0-3

Recipes

from

Pawleys Island

Revised Edition

RECIPES FROM PAWLEYS ISLAND

Church Women of
All Saints Waccamaw Episcopal Church
P.O. Box 69
Pawleys Island, SC 29585

All Saints, Waccamaw, is the ecclesiastical name for Waccamaw Neck, that Peninsula running over a score of miles along the Waccamaw River and between it and the ocean. It is blessed with fish and fowl and game. The recipes in this book reflect the outstanding meals that renowned social clubs and area plantations prided themselves with. Published in 1955, it is now in its 15th printing.

$ 6.95 Retail price
$ .35 Tax for South Carolina residents
$ 1.00 Postage and handling
Make check payable to All Saints Waccamaw Episcopal Church

SANDLAPPER COOKBOOK

Sandlapper Publishing Co., Inc.
P.O. Box 1932
Orangeburg, SC 29115   803/277-1673

The South has long been recognized for the high quality of its cuisine. Sandlapper has, since its beginning, reflected this culinary tradition by publishing recipes from some of South Carolina's best cooks. We offer them to you with the hope that they will provide many hours of cooking and eating pleasure.

$ 7.95 Retail price
$ .40 Tax for South Carolina residents
$ 1.25 Postage and handling
Make check payable to Sandlapper Publishing Co., Inc.
ISBN 0-87844-020-8

THE SANDLAPPERS' SALVATION COOKBOOK

Fairey Family Association
3011 Hickory Street
Burton, SC 29902   803/525-1544 or 525-3261

Sometimes called the "Geechee and Greek" cookbook, this is a collection of reunion recipes of the Fairey Family Association, which meets annually in Orangeburg, SC. (A "Geechee" is a native of the SC coast.) It contains 349 southern recipes with speical sections on Christmas, fig, pear, scuppernong grape and Greek recipes, county fair sweepstakes winners, and dietetic recipes. 126 pages.

$ 8.95 Retail price
$ .45 Tax for South Carolina residents
$ 1.50 Postage and handling
Make check payable to Martha Ann Tyree Moussatos

SEA ISLAND SEASONS

Beaufort County Open Land Trust
P.O. Box 75
Beaufort, SC 29901-0075   803/524-3121

Sea Island Seasons, a collaborative effort of the Beaufort County Open Land Trust, is a collection of over 700 favorite recipes of men and women of the South Carolina Low Country. It features tantalizing delicacies from generations of old family favorites. Now in it's fifth printing, it is sure to become one of your favorites.

$ 12.95 Retail price
$ .66 Tax for South Carolina residents
$ 1.75 Postage and handling
Make check payable to *Sea Island Seasons*
ISBN 0-918544-40-8

SEASONED WITH LIGHT

First Baptist Church - Baptist Women
Hartsville, SC 295520   803/332-6571

A charming book containing not only approximately 800 delicious recipes but lovely pen and ink drawings for dividers and brief regional history back of each drawing. The book is complete with direct newspaper and letter quotations from the mid 1800s. Nineteen recipe catagories including yesteryears, men's, seafood, diet and lite.

$ 10.00 Retail price
$ 2.00 Postage and handling
Make check payable to First Baptist Church (for Cookbook)

THE SOUTH CAROLINA COOK BOOK
(Revised Edition)

SC Extension Homemakers Council and the
Clemson Extension Home Economics Staff
University of South Carolina Press
1716 College Street
Columbia, SC 29208   803/777-5243

Now in its eighth printing since 1953, this book has been hailed by many as one of the most notable collections of Southern recipes and food customs. South Carolina's classic cookbook, it contains hundreds of recipes ranging from elementary to ambitious, and includes the favorite dishes of the Southern Appalachian peoples to those of the Carolina Lowcountry. 426 pages. Paperback.

$ 10.95 Retail price
$ .55 Tax for South Carolina residents
$ 2.00 Postage and handling
Make check payable to University of South Carolina Press
ISBN 0-87249-354-7

SOUTH CAROLINA'S HISTORIC RESTAURANTS AND THEIR RECIPES

John F. Blair, Publisher
1406 Plaza Drive
Winston-Salem, NC 27103

This book features fifty restaurants in South Carolina housed in buildings at least fifty years old. It also includes two or three recipes from each restaurant. This South Carolina entry is part of a series featuring seven southeastern states.

$ 12.95 Retail price
$ 1.50 Postage and handling
Make check payable to John F. Blair, Publisher
ISBN 0-89587-041-X

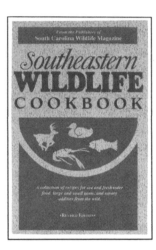

SOUTHEASTERN WILDLIFE COOKBOOK

South Carolina Wildlife Magazine
University of South Carolina Press
1716 College Street
Columbia, SC 29208   803/777-5243

Featuring more than 300 recipes that use wild game, fresh and saltwater foods, and some natural seasonings, this cookbook is for those who want to take the time to scout the woods and wetlands, as well as those who don't have time to but do have access to wild foods and want to serve them at their table. 224 pages, spiralbound.

$ 12.95 Retail price
$ .65 Tax for South Carolina residents
$ 2.00 Postage and handling
Make check payable to University of South Carolina Press
ISBN 0-87249-659-7

SOUTHERN COOKING

Sandlapper Publishing co.
P.O. Box 1932
Orangeburg, SC 29115   800/277-1673

Southern Cooking was formerly *The Columbia Sailing Club Cookbook*. With the growth of this impressive organization came the need to satisfy the hearty appetite stimulated by active racing. Through the years there have been recipes suitable for every sailing club occasion—from the sophisticated hors d'oeuvres of the Past Commodores Cocktail Party to cornbread and Hoppin' John.

$ 6.95 Retail price
$ .35 Tax for South Carolina residents
$ 1.25 Postage and handling
Make check payable to Sandlapper Publishing Co., Inc.
ISBN 0-87844-030-5

282

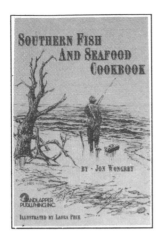

SOUTHERN FISH AND SEAFOOD COOKBOOK

Sandlapper Publishing Co., Inc.
P.O. Box 1932
Orangeburg, SC 29115   800/277-1673

The gentle art of southern fish cookery developed for the seafood enthusiast and compiled with the hopes of instilling the delight of catching and cooking fish. These recipes will assist in the preparation of a wide variety of seafood from the lightly browned and succulently baked to the savorily stewed.

$ 7.95 Retail price
$ .40 Tax for South Carolina residents
$ 1.25 Postage and handling
Make check payable to Sandlapper Publishing Co., Inc.
ISBN 0-87855-026-7

SOUTHERN VEGETABLE COOKING

Sandlapper Publishing Co., Inc.
P.O. Box 1932
Orangeburg, SC 29116   800/277-1673

A delightful cookbook composed to assist the inexperienced cook in the preparation of fresh vegetables. Particular emphasis is given to vegetables native to the South and prepared with a southern touch.

$ 7.95 Retail price
$ .40 Tax for South Carolina residents
$ 1.25 Postage and handling
Make check payable to Sandlapper Publishing Co., Inc.
ISBN 0-87844-045-3

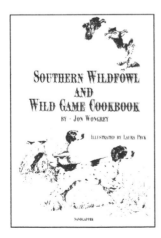

SOUTHERN WILDFOWL AND WILD GAME COOKBOOK

Sandlapper Publishing Co., Inc.
P.O. Box 1932
Orangeburg, SC 29115   800/277-1673

A collection of savory game recipes prepared for both wildfowl and animals with emphasis on the individual qualities of wild game. This cookbook begins with field preparation of game and continues with kitchen preparation on the basic know-how of game cooking.

$ 7.95 Retail price
$ .40 Tax for South Carolina residents
$ 1.25 Postage and handling
Make check payable to Sandlapper Publishing Co., Inc.
ISBN 0-87844-035-6

STIR CRAZY

Junior League of Florence, SC Inc.
P.O. Box 3715
Florence, SC 29502-0715   803/667-0376

All recipes are twice-tested, and the book has a cross-referenced index. Chosen for inclusion in *America's Best: A Hometown Collection* this year. Gourmet recipes, quick and easy recipes, Southern traditional recipes. Something for everyone. 560 recipes, 14 food sections, 328 total pages.

$ 12.95 Retail price
$ .65 Tax for South Carolina residents
$ 2.00 Postage and handling
Make check payable to Junior League of Florence
ISBN 0-9615863-0-3

STIRRIN' THE POTS ON DAUFUSKIE

by Billie Burn
P.O. Box 29
Daufuskie Island, SC 29915   803/842-1294

Stirrin' The Pots On Daufuskie consists of 197 pages of pictures and household hints with bits of history woven in with lowcountry recipes, some of which are written in Gullah. From Cracked Crab Gravy to Oyster Purlo, its uniqueness has resulted in 11,000 copies. Now in its third printing.

$ 8.50 Retail price
$ 1.50 Postage and handling
Make check payable to Billie Burn Books
ISBN 0-9614670-0-2

STRICTLY FOR BOYS

by Betty L. Waskiewicz
P.O. Box 474/2312 Depot Road
Beaufort, SC 29901   803/524-2843

Great little book written *"Strictly For Boys"* and is just that—good food which boys will enjoy cooking as well as eating. Divided into sections according to difficulty. Nice gift for anyone "new" in the kitchen.

$ 7.95 Retail price
$ .40 Tax for South Carolina residents
$ 1.25 Postage and handling
Make check payable to *Strictly For Boys*
ISBN 0-918544-47-5

A TASTE OF SOUTH CAROLINA

Sandlapper Publishing Co., Inc.
P.O. Box 1932
Orangeburg, SC 29115   800/277-1673

A collection of recipes contributed by the Palmetto Cabinet (its members, legislators, governors, U.S. Senators, congressmen, constitutional officers, and many South Carolinians). Recipes vary from those of the Governor's Mansion, home of South Carolina's first family, to menus suitable for various types of entertaining including selection of proper wines.

$ 11.95 Retail price
$ .60 Tax for South Carolina residents
$ 1.25 Postage and handling
Make check payable to Sandlapper Publishing Co., Inc.
ISBN 0-87844-064-X

THOROUGHBRED FARE COOKBOOK

200 Hartwell Drive
Aiken, SC 29801   803/649-43340 or 648-2744

The *Thoroughbred Fare* cookbook, 250 pages with 400 tested recipes, reflects the culture and lifestyle of Aiken, a city famous for its horses and polo. The delightful blend of tasty recipes, pen and ink drawings and historical tidbits includes a special section of tailgating recipes for the races or football games.

$ 9.95 Retail price
$ .60 Tax for South Carolina residents
$ 2.00 Postage and handling
Make check payable to *Thoroughbred Fare Cookbook*

TWO HUNDRED YEARS OF CHARLESTON COOKING

University of South Carolina Press
1716 College Street
Columbia, SC 29208   803/777-5243

This well-known cookbook contains 307 magnificent tradtional Charleston "receipts." Especially valuable for its rice and seafood recipes, it's also spiced with Charleston gossip. 289 pages, clothbound and paperback.

$ 19.95 Retail price (cloth) $10.95 (paper)
$ 1.00 Tax for South Carolina residents; ¢.55 paper
$ 2.00 Postage and handling
Make check payable to University of South Carolina Press
ISBN 0-87249-346-6 (cloth) and 0-87249-348-2 (paper)

UPTOWN DOWN SOUTH

Junior League of Greenville
17 W. North Street
Greenville, SC 29601   803/232-1286

Uptown Down South is a collection of menus containing over 400 triple-tested recipes. Each menu has been planned with special attention to taste, appearance and recipe comparability. Menus ranging from the uptown elegance of gourmet dinners to the down south casual dining on the patio take you from morning to midday and into the evening.

$ 11.95 Retail price
$ .60 Tax for South Carolina residents
$ 2.00 Postage and handling
Make check payable to Junior League of Greenville
ISBN 0-960817212

Preserving America's Food Heritage

"BEST of the BEST" Cookbook Series

Best of the Best from **ALABAMA** 288 pages, $16.95	**Best of the Best from** **INDIANA** 288 pages, $16.95	**Best of the Best from** **MISSISSIPPI** 288 pages, $16.95	**Best of the Best from** **PENNSYLVANIA** 320 pages, $16.95
Best of the Best from **ARKANSAS** 288 pages, $16.95	**Best of the Best from** **IOWA** 288 pages, $16.95	**Best of the Best from** **MISSOURI** 304 pages, $16.95	**Best of the Best from** **SOUTH CAROLINA** 288 pages, $16.95
Best of the Best from **COLORADO** 288 pages, $16.95	**Best of the Best from** **KENTUCKY** 288 pages, $16.95	**Best of the Best from** **NEW ENGLAND** 368 pages, $16.95	**Best of the Best from** **TENNESSEE** 288 pages, $16.95
Best of the Best from **FLORIDA** 288 pages, $16.95	**Best of the Best from** **LOUISIANA** 288 pages, $16.95	**Best of the Best from** **NEW MEXICO** 288 pages, $16.95	**Best of the Best from** **TEXAS** 352 pages, $16.95
Best of the Best from **GEORGIA** 336 pages, $16.95	**Best of the Best from** **LOUISIANA II** 288 pages, $16.95	**Best of the Best from** **NORTH CAROLINA** 288 pages, $16.95	**Best of the Best from** **TEXAS II** 352 pages, $16.95
Best of the Best from the **GREAT PLAINS** 288 pages, $16.95	**Best of the Best from** **MICHIGAN** 288 pages, $16.95	**Best of the Best from** **OHIO** 352 pages, $16.95	**Best of the Best from** **VIRGINIA** 320 pages, $16.95
Best of the Best from **ILLINOIS** 288 pages, $16.95	**Best of the Best from** **MINNESOTA** 288 pages, $16.95	**Best of the Best from** **OKLAHOMA** 288 pages, $16.95	**Best of the Best from** **WISCONSIN** 288 pages, $16.95

Cookbooks listed above have been completed as of January 1, 2000.

Special discount offers available!

(See previous page for details.)

To order by credit card, call toll-free **1-800-343-1583** or send check or money order to:
QUAIL RIDGE PRESS • P. O. Box 123 • Brandon, MS 39043
Visit our website at **www.quailridge.com** to order online!

- -

 # Order form

Send completed form and payment to:
QUAIL RIDGE PRESS • P. O. Box 123 • Brandon, MS 39043

❑ Check enclosed

Charge to: ❑ Visa ❑ MasterCard
❑ Discover ❑ American Express

Card # _____

Expiration Date _____

Signature _____

Name _____

Address_____

City/State/Zip_____

Phone #_____

Qty.	Title of Book (State)		Total
		SubTotal	_____
		7% Tax for MS residents	_____
		Postage ($3.00 any number of books)	+ 3.00
		Total	_____